Table Tennis

Second Edition

Ya-ping Wang
Shenyang Institute of Physical Education, China

Gong Chen, Ed.D.
San Jose State University, USA

Copley Custom Textbooks

An imprint of XanEdu Custom Publishing

ISBN 13: 978-1-59399-223-1
ISBN 10: 1-59399-223-8
Reprinted January 2010

Copley Custom Textbooks
An imprint of XanEdu Publishing, Inc.
138 Great Road
Acton, Massachusetts 01720
800-562-2147

Please visit our Web site at www.xanedu.com/copley

Dedication

This book is

Dedicated

To

Our family members
For their
Forever love and support

And to

Our former professors and teachers

Contents

Part Two. Major Skills and strategies

Preface

Since table tennis became an official Olympic sport in 1988, it is getting more popular in the United States and in the world. The International Table Tennis Federation has 186 countries and areas as its members. In the United States, it is also becoming a popular sport and activity, especially Asian minority communities, sport clubs and community centers, colleges and universities, and in some high schools and middle schools. In many cities, special table tennis clubs have been established to training youth for higher level competitions in the United States.

This book is written for middle school, high school, college, and university table tennis courses at beginning and intermediate levels in the United States. It is also can be used by table tennis fans and amateur players. As China is starting bilingual education at university level, this book can serve as a good reference used with Chinese table tennis books for bilingual education in table tennis courses in Chinese colleges and universities as well.

The second edition of this book has been designed to provide students a comprehensive view of table tennis. It includes two parts. The first part briefly discusses table tennis history, benefits, different levels of players and training features, major organizations and competition, basic table tennis rules and etiquette, dressing and equipment, warm-up, and prevention of injuries. The second part introduces basic stances, grips, footwork, different serves and returns, different shots and application features, and single and double game strategies.

This book has been written to use simple languages to introduce knowledge and skills. The authors' teaching experience indicated that keeping the text simple will help students more effectively remember the key facts of what they learned with less confusion. For example, the history part is just a list and the benefits section is also a simple list. This book also reduces the contents on rules by introducing the necessary contents only. This not only reduces students' reading time but also help them focus more on important facts.

We hope this book will help students in the United States learn table tennis better and enjoy table tennis as a great lifetime activity. We also hope this book will help students in China get familiar with table tennis terms and applications in English at the same time they learn table tennis. Any feedback can go to gongchen@kin.sjsu.edu.

Authors

January 2006

Acknowledgments

We wish to express our great gratitude to

Gloria Hsu

For her excellent contribution of computer designs in the book

and

Heather Terbeek

For reading and editing from a reader's perspective

Chapter 1

History, benefits, players, organizations, and major competitions

This chapter will introduce a brief history and present status of table tennis. The benefits of playing table tennis will be introduced briefly as well. To make the learning easy, all contents in this chapter will be introduced in a list format. This chapter will also introduce different levels of players and their training characteristics, and major table tennis competitions and organizations in the world. The purpose is to provide students a brief overview of the highest level of table tennis competitions and professional organizations in a big picture.

Brief history

1. Table tennis is commonly recognized to have started in England although there are different opinions.

2. It is commonly accepted that table tennis originated from tennis in 1800s. When the weather was too poor to play tennis outside, some people used rubber or cork balls and constructed an imitation of tennis to play on a table as a game.

3. In 1890, a player brought back a toy ball made of celluloid from the United States to England and used it in table tennis activities. Because the celluloid ball sounds like *ping* and *pong* when it is hit with the paddle, it was also called Ping Pong.

4. In the beginning of 1900s, table tennis spread to other European and Asian countries.

5. After 1918 when World War I ended, table tennis gained popularity in Europe and so many countries began to establish table tennis associations. At the same time, competitions in table tennis increased among theses countries while people invented and improved equipment. As the skill and competition level improved, players decided that they needed to organize a governing body for table tennis.

6. In December of 1926, the International Table Tennis Federation and competition rules for playing table tennis were established. Table tennis thus became an official international sport.

7. From 1920s through 1950s, European countries took the leadership of table tennis in the world. The game was slow and the major style was defensive play.

8. In the 1950s, the sponge paddle was invented in Japan. This new invention made the shots much faster and Japan took four champions in 1952 using this type of paddles.

9. In the beginning of 1960s, China became a leading table tennis country.

10. After the 1970s, the European countries with the loop style and Asian countries with a fast style took turns to lead table tennis trends.

11. The "Diplomatic Ping Pong" ended the cold war between the United States and China in 1971.

12. Table tennis became an official Olympic sport in 1988 in Seoul, Korea.

13. Many players combined the advantages of all styles together to make games more competitive and exciting.

14. After the Sidney Olympic Games in 2000, the International Table Tennis Federation changed the size of the ball from 38 millimeters to 40 millimeters in order to slow down the game and make the games more fun to the spectators as an effort to promote table tennis market.

15. Due to the change of rules, more countries have chances to win the medals at world-class competitions. However, the top players have more chances to lose their games.

16. The pen grip style came back strongly at the 2004 Athens Olympic Games. Both men's single champion and second place used the pen grip. The champion used the traditional pen grip and the second place used new pen grip.

Present status

1. Table tennis is not a very popular sport in high schools or colleges/universities in the United States, and only a few universities have table tennis classes. Table tennis in the United States is mainly practiced at the club level and most of all in some minority communities. As a result, the competition level in table tennis games in the United States is not very high.

2. Table tennis is most popular in many Asian countries and areas, and European countries. In the world, the leading country is still China and it took four out of five gold medals in recent World Championship in May of 2003, and three out of four champions in the 2004 Athens Olympic Games. There are world level players in China, South Korea, North Korea, Taiwan, and Japan. The countries that have world-class players in Europe include Sweden, France, Austria, and Germany.

3. Table tennis will gradually get more popular in the United States and around the world because of its status as an Olympic sport and its benefits to the health. This will be particularly difficult for table tennis in the United States in the near future due to competition with other sports that involve monetary gains, have established their market, and have longer-standing traditions (such as basketball, softball, football, tennis, and volleyball).

Benefits of table tennis

Playing table tennis can benefit players in many ways based research and practical experience. Table tennis benefits people of all ages and abilities. It also can be played in a competitive way or a recreational way. The benefits range from physical to spiritual aspects. The following benefits are listed in a concrete way for people to remember.

1. Mental aspects:

1) Establish an overall understanding of how table tennis can be used to enrich one's personal life.
2) Learn mental strategies of table tennis that can be used in everyday life and at work.

2. Social aspects:

1) Learn the social rules, manners, and etiquette in table tennis that can be applied in daily life.
2) Learn to work and communicate with partners and opponents in the gym setting.

3. Emotional aspects:

1) Develop a tough mind for potential hard life in the future.
2) Develop the ability to push yourself to reach your life goals.
3) Release stress in an unharmed way.

4. Spiritual aspects:

1) Develop self-confidence and spirit for self-actualization.
2) Develop competitive spirit that is needed in a competitive society.

5. Practical aspects:

1) Improve body appearance.
2) Improve performance at work and in everyday life.
3) Improve body metabolism (burn calories and improve appetite).

6. Medical aspects:

1) Prevent muscle atrophy and osteoporosis.
2) Slow down the aging process.
3) Reduce fat.
4) Prevent and treat high blood pressure.
5) Prevent heart diseases.
6) Prevent and treat diabetes

7. Health-related fitness:

1) Improve muscular strength.
2) Improve muscular endurance
3) Improve cardiovascular endurance.
4) Improve muscular flexibility.

8. Skill-related fitness:

1) Improve explosive power.
2) Improve endurance.
3) Improve agility.
4) Improve flexibility.
5) Improve speed.
6) Improve coordination.
7) Improve reaction time.

Motivate yourself and others to play table tennis

1. Understand the benefits you can receive from table tennis.
2. Find a good place to play.
3. Find a supportive group to play together.
4. Learn and practice to make yourself play better and enjoy it.
5. Look at your achievement and results of playing table tennis.
6. Enjoy the process.
7. Set up goals and objectives and make a time just for table tennis.

Different levels of players and their training features

   Table tennis is played at different skill and competition levels for different purposes. It ranges from backyard or garage recreational table tennis to club practice and competition, to school competition, to professional training and competitions. At each level, players play with different styles and train differently. This chapter will briefly introduce the specific features of each level of play and practice. A good understanding of these levels and features will help you make proper decisions on where to start and which way to go for further participation in table tennis.

1. Backyard or garage players

   Who: Anyone who just plays for fun at backyard or in the garage
   Purposes:
   - Convenient exercise
   - Family recreation
   - Social activity
   - Development of interest for sport and activity for children

   Training features:
   1) No formal skills required
   2) No rules needed
   3) Play just for fun, exercise, or recreation
   4) Light activity or low impact exercise

2. Beginners (getting-the-foot-wet players)

Who: Players who want to learn formal skills and rules
Purposes:
- Try table tennis as a sport option
- Want to play real table tennis
- Want to join a club or team
- To use table tennis as a lifetime sport or exercise

Training features:
1) Train with an instructor or a coach
2) Start with formal basic skills
3) Learn basic rules
4) Learn how to apply skills and rules in easy games
5) Learn basic and simple drills to develop skills
6) Beginning level of exercise intensity

3. Intermediate players (serious players)

Who: People who learned basic skills, rules, and play; and want to play better
Purposes:
- To continuously develop table tennis as a lifetime sport
- To play better games in tournament competitions
- To become a real table tennis player
- To use table tennis as a high impact exercise

Training features:
1) Improve basic skills and applications
2) Learn intermediate skills
3) Play more effective games
4) Learn strategies
5) Participate in tournaments
6) Intermediate intensity of training

4. Advanced players and coaches

Who: People who can perform regular skills and play games effectively
Purposes:
- To play more competitive games in tournaments
- To become a high level player
- To use table tennis as a daily exercise
- To continuously develop table tennis as a lifetime sport

Training features:
1) Improve speed, power, and placement
2) Combination skills
3) More variations of skills and applications
4) Specific training on each skills and strategies
5) Play in higher level tournaments

6) Better observation skills
7) More strategies
8) Develop personal playing styles
9) Coach other people at beginning level

5. Pre-professional players

Who: People who want to become professional players for high level games
Purposes:
- To practice and play for professional tournaments
- To become a professional player
- To choose table tennis as a career
- To make money and fame in table tennis

Training features:
1) Improve efficiency of skills
2) Better body conditioning
3) Psychological training
4) Specific training on skills and tactics
5) Skill and strategy flexibility in play
6) More professional tournaments
7) Coach other people at intermediate level

6. Professional players

Who: People who want to be the best player in table tennis
Purposes:
- To practice and play in professional tournaments
- To become a top player in the nation and the world
- To represent their countries for top tournaments
- To make money and gain fame in table tennis

Training features:
1) Perfect skills and strategies
2) Hard body conditioning training
3) Stress on mental training
4) Participate in national/world level competitions
5) Imitate the top players from the other countries for the team practice and preparation
6) Specific training targeting at each world level opponents

Major organizations

1. The world

Name: International Table Tennis Federation (ITTF)

Functions: Governing table tennis activities in the world
    1) Promote table tennis in the world
    2) Establish and uphold laws of table tennis
    3) Arrange world level tournaments
    4) Sanction tournaments in the world
Members: 186 countries and areas, including

Africa	39
Asia	42
Europe	55
Latin America	32
North America	4
Oceania	14

2. The United States

Name: USA Table Tennis
Functions: Governing table tennis activities in the U.S.
    1) Promote table tennis in the United States
    2) Establish and uphold laws of table tennis
    3) Arrange national and open tournaments
    4) Sanction tournaments at different levels
    5) Represent U.S. in international competitions and other activities.

Major competitions

There are several levels of competitions in the world. The highest level of table tennis tournaments includes the World Championship, the Olympic Games, the Pro Tour, and the World Cup. The second level includes continental championships, such as Asian championship and Asian games, different opens (e.g. U.S. Open, China Open, England Open, etc.). The third level tournaments include world youth championship and continental youth championship. The player who receives the highest score will be the annual champion. In this chapter, the four top world tournaments will be introduced.

1. World Championship

1) Origin: Started in 1926
2) Time: Held in every two years (odd years only)
3) Events:
- Men's team (separate from single events in 2003)
- Women's team (separate from single events in 2003)
- Men's single
- Women's single
- Men' double
- Women's double
- Mixed double

4) Awards for the permanent Championship trophies:
- The Swaythling Cup for the men's team event
- The Marcel Corbillon Cup for the women's team event
- The St Bride Vase for the men's singles event
- The G Geist Prize for the women's singles event
- The Iran Cup for the men's doubles event
- The W J Pope Trophy for the women's doubles event
- The Heydusek prize for the mixed doubles event

2. World Cup

1) Origin: Started in 1980
2) Time: Held annually
3) Events: Separate Tournaments for Men's singles and women's singles only.
4) Participants: Only 16 players for each men's and women's tournaments, including:
- The current holder of the World Cup
- The champion player or the strongest current player from each of the six continents
- one player from the host Association
- the top 6 players from the World Ranking List
- two "wild card" selections
5) Participants will be provided with free return travel tickets to the venue and with free meals and accommodation from dinner on the evening before the start of the competition to breakfast on the morning after it ends.

3. Olympic

1) Origin: Started in 1988
2) Time: Held every four years
3) Events:

Men's single	64 players
Women's single	48 players
Men's double	32 pairs
Women's double	16 pairs

4) Matches: All games play best four games out of seven

4. ITTF Pro Tour Grant Finals

1) Origin: Started in 1996
2) Time: Held annually at the end of every year
3) Events:

Men's single	16 players
Women's single	16 players
Men's double	8 pairs
Women's double	8 pairs

4) Match: All games play best four games out of seven

5. Other regional competitions

    1) Continental Championships
    2) Opens (such as U.S. Open, France Open, China Open, e.g.)

Review questions

1. Where was table tennis invented by common opinion?
2. How was the name "Ping Pong" adopted?
3. When was the ITTF established?
4. When and where was the sponge paddle invented?
5. When did table tennis become an Olympic game?
6. What was the "Diplomatic Ping Pong" and when did it happen?
7. When did ITTF change the size of the ball and why?
8. At which level and in which groups is table tennis popular in the U.S.?
9. Which countries have world level table tennis players?
10. Which country is still the strongest at table tennis?
11. What can table tennis benefit people in terms of the mental aspect?
12. What can table tennis benefit people in terms of the emotional aspect?
13. What can table tennis benefit people in terms of the spiritual aspect?
14. What can table tennis benefit people in terms of the social aspect?
15. What can table tennis benefit people in terms of the medical aspect?
16. What can table tennis benefit people in terms of the practical aspect?
17. What can table tennis benefit people in terms of the health aspect?
18. What can table tennis benefit people in terms of the fitness aspect?
19. What are the major purposes and training characteristics of backyard or garage table tennis players?
20. What are the major purposes and training characteristics of beginning table tennis players?
21. What are the major purposes and training characteristics of intermediate level table tennis players?
22 What are the major purposes and training characteristics of advanced level table tennis players?
23. What are the major purposes and training characteristics of pre-professional level table tennis players?
24. What are the major purposes and training characteristics of professional table tennis players?
25. What is the name of the table tennis governing body in the world and how many members it has?
26. What is the name of the table tennis governing body in the United States?
27. How often is the World Championship Game held?
28. How many events are there in the World Championship Game?
29. What is the Swaythling Cup for?
30. What is the Marcel Corbilon Cup for?
31. What is the St Bride Case for?

32. What is the G Geist Prize for?
33. How often is the World Cup held and how many players participate?
34. When did table tennis become one of an Olympic event?
35. When is the Pro Tour Grant Final held?

Chapter 2

Basic simplified rules and etiquette

This chapter will introduce basic rules and etiquette of table tennis. Rules that are practical for regular classes will be introduced in a simplified way so that students will understand and remember these rules easily. The comprehensive rules for table tennis can be found on the ITTF's and USATT's websites.

Legal serves

Solution: Game continues when the server follows the following rules...

1. The server holds the ball on the open palm.
2. Toss vertically up no less than 16 centimeters without spin.
3. Hit the ball only when the ball is coming down from the toss.
4. The ball and paddle both are above the table at the contact.
5. The ball should be behind the baseline of the table.
6. The ball hits the server's table first, and then the receiver's table.
7. The receiver should have a clear view of server's ball and paddle.
8. The ball needs to go over or around the net.
9. Warning for the first violation, and one point penalty for the second and after.

Illegal serves

Solution: Receiver gets a point if the server violates any of the following rules...

1. The server misses the ball when serving.
2. The ball does not hit the server's side first.
3. The ball hits the server's side but does not hit receiver's table.
4. The ball hit the server's side more than once.
5. The ball does not go over the net after it bounces once on the server's side.
6. The server hides the ball.
7. The server hits below the table.
8. The server hits above the table between the baseline and the net.
9. The server does not toss the ball high enough.

Legal returns

Solution: Game continues if the receiver follows the following rules...

1. The receiver of a serve or shot has to return the ball after it bounces on the receiver's side once only and before twice.
2. The receiver has to hit the ball over or around the net into opponent's table after hitting the ball.

Illegal returns/shots

Solution: The hitter's opponent gets a point if the hitter violates any of the following rules...

1. The hitter fails to hit the ball after it bounces once and before it bounces twice on his/her side.
2. The ball fails to reach opponent's table after it is hit.
3. The ball fails to go over the net after it is hit.
4. The hitter hits the ball before it bounces on the table.
5. The ball touches the outside textures (ceiling, floor) after the hitter hits it.
6. The hitter touches the ball more than once.
7. The hitter's cloths or body moves the table.
8. The hitter or cloths or paddle touch the net.
9. The hitter's open hand hits the table.
10. The player who is hit by the ball after the ball hits his/her table.
11. Out of the order hit in doubles.

Let

Solution: Re-serve the point when any of the following situation occur...

1. The ball touches the net in serves then gets over (if the ball gets over and lands on the receiver's right side in double games, it is a let, but it is a fault if it lands on the left side).
2. The receiver is not ready to receive.
3. Interferences (such as someone walks too close to the receiver).
4. The referee stops the game.

Toss, change end, and match (how to play the game)

1. Toss a coin (or guess the ball) to determine the winner of the toss.
2. The winner can choose serve or side and the loser picks up the leftover.
3. The players switch their ends after each game.
4. One game is 11 points. Any player who gets 11 points first and leads the opponent by at least two points wins the game unless the scores tie at 10:10, in which one player has to win two points to win the game.
5. An international match usually plays best four out of seven games. Some tournaments may play best two out of three, or best three out of five.

Single serving order and hitting order

1. One player makes two serves in a row, and then the opponent makes two serves.
2. When both sides tie at 10:10, each side makes one serve only until one side leads by two points, and then the game is over.

3. The server can serve from any corner of the table and serve to any part of the opponent's table.

4. If a player starts the first serve in the first game, then the opponent should serve first in the second game.

5. Then the first server in the first game serves first in the third game and the opponent serves in the fourth game. Both sides continuously serve in this order until the end of the match.

6. The server serves, then the receiver hits back, then the server hits. Continuously hit in this order until one side loses the rally.

Double serve order and hitting order

The first game

1. The serving side should determine the first server (S1) and receiving side determines the first receiver (R1) before the match starts. Then the server's partner should be S2 and the receiver's partner should be R2.

2. This game should follow this serving order: S1 serves to R1 twice, then R1 serves to S2 twice, then S2 serves to R2 twice, then R2 serves to S1 twice (S1 → R1→ S2 → R2 → S1). Continue until the end of the game.

3. The hitting order is same as the serving order. R1 returns S1's serve, then S2 returns R1's shot, then R2 returns S2's shot, then S1 returns R2's shot. Continue until the end of the game.

4. Every time the serve is switched, the former receiver should become the server, and the server's partner becomes the receiver.

The second game and the following games

1. The receiving side of the first game will serve first in the second game and they should determine the first server. Any player of the serving side can serve first. After the first server is decided, then the serving order of this game is determined.

2. The first receiver must be the player who in the prior game served to the first server in the second game. If R1 is the first server in the second game, then the first receiver should be S1 (S1 served to R1 in the prior game). Then the serving and hitting order in the second game should be R1 → S1 → R2 → S2 → R1. If R2 wants to serve first in the second game, then the first receiver should be S2 (S2 served and hit to R2 in the prior game). Then the serving and hitting order in the second game should be R2 → S2 → R1 → A1 → R2.

3. The third game and the following game should follow the model of the second game. Any player in the serving side can serve first.

Special double game serving and hitting rules

1. The server in double game can only serve from the right side of his/her table diagonally to the receiver's right side of the table. A serve touching the centerline is counted as "in".

2. If the server serves from left side of the centerline or serves to the left side of the opponent's centerline, the server loses a point.

3. When the server serves to the receiver, the receiver has to return the serve. If the receiver's partner returns the server, the receiving side loses a point.

Etiquette of table tennis

Each sport has its own personality, out of which grows its etiquette (usage of polite society) and procedures (manner of proceeding and acting). The possibility of negative feelings increases and the enjoyable atmosphere is ruined if common etiquette and procedures are not followed when playing without a referee. That is not the way people want to play since table tennis is a friendly game. If you do not follow the etiquette, you will find that nobody wants to play with you anymore and you will lose your position in table tennis. To become a skilled table tennis player, one should learn how to be a good player first. The following aspects will help you become a good player.

1. In classes

1) Come to class on time.
2) Set up and take off the tables.
3) Retrieve your balls instead of waiting for your partner or opponent to do it.
4) Take care of facility and equipment.
5) Respect the instructor and classmates.
6) Never walk close to the table when other people are practicing or playing.

2. In practice

1) Do not select partners since that will limit your experience and hurt other people.
2) Introduce yourself to your partner and opponent so that you know each other better.
3) Follow the class schedule. Discuss with your partner if your want to do more advanced or complicated drills.
4) Accept latecomers.
5) Do your best at anytime.
6) Encourage and help each other.

3. During warm-up

1) Share your table and control the ball placement in your boundary.
2) Hit the ball that you can control.
3) If you lose the ball in another court, do not run or sneak into there to get it back. Wait until people on that side finish the rally or wait until they pick it up for you.
4) Ask your partner and/or opponent if they are ready to start the game.
5) Keep the ball in rally and do not showoff at this time.

4. Before the match

1) Make arrangement about the balls.
2) Decide on specific rules in disagreement when playing without referees.
3) Decide who will start.

5. During the match

1) Remember the purpose of table tennis when you play games. Enjoyment and prevention of injuries should always come before winning or losing. No point is worth winning if you or your opponent are injured or get negative feelings.
2) Both the server and receiver should be ready for the service.
3) Call score and wait until your partner/opponent is ready before serving.
4) Retrieve the ball on your side.
5) When returning the ball to your opponent for service, hit the bird directly over the net with easy motion.
6) Call your fault promptly, fairly, and clearly.
7) Call in favor of your opponent or replay the point if you are not sure if the shot is in or out.
8) Follow the general rules. Talk it and play it over if there is any disagreement.
9) Make calls on your side and your opponent calls on his/her side. Never question your opponent's call by looking or words.
10) Suggest a replay if opponent is handicapped by unusual interference.
11) Compliment your opponent on his/her exceptionally good shots after the rally is over.
12) Emotional tantrum such as throwing your paddle or using foul language has no place in the game of table tennis. The customary lack of such display is one of the things that make table tennis so attractive to players and spectators alike.
13) Do not blame your partner for making mistakes in games. He/she needs more encouragement for better plays. Remember everybody makes mistakes.
14) Always play your best game. Careless play is an insult to your opponent and partner.

6. After the match

1) Shake hands with your partner and opponent, thank them for the game, and compliment their play.
2) Discuss the game and get some feedback.
3) Be a good loser and humble winner.

7. Bad manners to avoid

1) Lack of respect to opponent or referees.
2) Bad talks such as yelling, swearing, or using bad language.
3) Getting angry with people easily.
4) Throwing the paddle, banging on the table, and hitting the ball with deadly force while the ball is not in play.
5) Arrogant attitude to opponent.
6) Never picking up the ball and always waiting for the opponent to do it.
7) Laughing at people's mistakes.

Reviewing questions

Serves

1. What is the minimum height the server must toss the ball when serving?
2. Can the server hit the ball when it is tossed up?
3. Can the server serve below the table?
4. Can the server serve right over the table between the baseline and the net?
5. What is the penalty when the server's ball touches opponent's side first?
6. What is the penalty when the ball hits the server's side and then scratches opponent's table edge?
7. What is the penalty for an illegal serve?
8. Can the server hide the ball behind the body when delivering the serve?
9. What is the penalty when the server's ball touches the net and gets over?

Shots

1. What is the penalty when a player makes an illegal shot?
2. What is the penalty when a player hits the ball before it touches his/her table?
3. What is the penalty when the ball hits the player's paddle behind the baseline?
4. What is the penalty when the ball touches the net and gets over in a rally?
5. What is the penalty when a player's open hand pounds the table during a rally?
6. What is the penalty when a player's shot goes around the net and gets in?
7. What is the penalty when a player hits the ball after it bounces twice?
8. What is the penalty when the ball hits a player after the ball hits his table?

Lets

1. What is the penalty for a "let"?
2. What is the penalty for a serve in which the ball touches the net and gets over?
3. What is the penalty for a serve in which the ball touches the net and gets over the other side of the table down in a doubles game?
4. What is the penalty for serving the ball before the opponent is ready?
5. What should be called when a player bumps into a spectator behind him in games?

Games

1. What is the common way to determine the choices for serve or end?
2. When should players switch ends in matches?
3. How many points for a single game?
4. How many points for a doubles game?
5. What should both sides do when they tie at 10:10?
6. What many games are usually played in each match?

Singles

1. How many serves can a player make in a row during singles games?
2. Can the server serve to or from any corner he/she wants in a singles game?
3. Who should serve first in the second game?
4. Who should serve first in the third game?
5. How many serves should each player take based on the new rules?

Doubles

1. Which player of the serving side can make the first serve in the first game?
2. Which player should serve in the second game?
3. What is the serving and receiving order in the first game?
4. Who should be the first receiver in the second game?
5. After the server performs two serves, who should be the next server?
6. Which player should serve first in the third game?
7. What is the penalty when the server serves from the left side of the table?
8. What is the penalty when the server serves from the right side down the table?
9. What is the penalty when the receiver's partner returns the serve?

Etiquette

1. What is the proper manner when taking classes?
2. What is the common etiquette during the practice period?
3. What is the proper manner during the warm-up process?
4. What is the proper behavior in competitions?
5. What kind of behavior

Chapter 3

Dress, equipment, and warm-up

This chapter will briefly introduce proper dress and selection of equipment, the warm-up guidelines and activities. These guidelines are general basic guidelines for everybody, but each player can and should also develop his/her own style of warm-up and cool-down process. This chapter will also introduce common injuries in table tennis, basic principles of injury prevention, and basic treatment for injuries.

Dress and supplies recommended

Dressing properly for table tennis can make your movement easy and reduce the chance of injuries. Dressing in table tennis attire will also make your look and feel good, and make your partner and opponents feel respected. You will have better and friendlier practice and competitions with proper attire. Proper equipment is also important to practice and games.

1. A couple of paddles
2. Celluloid table tennis balls
3. Shorts and sport shirt
4. Warm-up suite for cold weather
5. Court shoes, low heel and relative thin sole recommended for safety and easy movement.
6. Extra shirts and shocks for change
7. Towels
8. Drinking water

Equipment and selection

Brands   There are different manufactures for table tennis paddles and balls. The famous brands include Red Double Happiness, Butterfly, etc. Professional players usually have their own preferences for paddles, but for amateur players, any brand will work well.

Rubbers   There are two different types of rubbers people use on their paddles. One type is pimpled rubber and another is reverse pimpled rubber. The pimpled rubber (Photo 3.1) allows more power but less spin and it is good for flats shots. It is mainly for the close-table fast style players. The reverse pimpled rubber (Photo 3.2) has less power but more spin motion and it is good for topspin and backspin shots. It can be used for defensive players (players who use more slice shots) and loop type of players (players who use more loop shots). Some players use pimpled on one side and reverse pimpled on the other side to allow more variety of shots and to confuse opponent with spin and no-spin serves and shots.

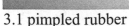
3.1 pimpled rubber   3.2 reverse pimpled rubber

Handles   There are two types of handles on the paddles (Photo 3.3). One (the left paddle in Photo 3.3) is short and is used by the "Pen-grip" type players. Another (the right paddle one in Photo 3.3) is longer and is used by the "Tennis-grip" type players. The close-table, fast, and strong forehand players tend to use the pen-grip paddle. On the other hand, powerful, off-table, strong on forehand and backhand players tend to use more tennis-grip.

3.3 comparisons of short and long handles

Warm-up and cool-down

Warm-up and cool-down are two important parts of table tennis. The warm-up is performed before the practice/game and the cool-down is performed after. Warm-up activities can prevent potential injuries and prepare your body for effective practice and games. Cool-down activities can reduce the after-workout problems, prevent muscle bound, and help recover quickly from the practice and games and get ready for next day's practice or games.

There is a misunderstanding on the terms and the contents of warm-up. People (including many coaches) tend to use the word "stretching" as the warm-up. This often misleads the players to stretch their muscles only and forget other activities, especially those concerning joints. The joints are much vulnerable to injuries than muscles and usually take much longer time to recover if they are injured. Some joint injuries can become a permanent problem and cannot be healed.

The warm-up process is individualized based on personal preferences. Each player may have his or her own styles for warm-ups. Generally warm-ups should follow a certain pattern so that players do not skip any body part. The following four types of activities are considered as a comprehensive warm-up, but the specific activities for each type of movement can be different.

1. Major warm-up activities

    1) Stretching activities: to prepare all muscle groups to be used
    2) Rotating activities: to prepare all joints to be involved
    3) Running or jumping activities: to warm the muscles and raise the heart rate
    4) Footwork and swinging motions

2. A warm-up process example

The stretching and rotation procedures can be combined together to follow a certain pattern. The common way is to start with the neck muscle and joint, then to gradually go down to ankle and toes. It also can do the reverse way from ankles to the neck. The following is am example of this type of warm-up:

    1) stretch the neck front back and forth, then sideways
    2) rotate shoulders in circular motions
    3) rotate elbows and wrists
    4) rotate fingers
    5) lean forward and backward to stretch upper-back and low-back
    6) rotate hip joints
    7) stretch hamstring and quadriceps
    8) rotate knees
    9) stretch calf muscles
    10) rotate ankles and toes
    11) run or run in place
    12) easy footwork
    13) easy swings

3. A good cool-down process should include the following activities:

    1) Relax all muscle groups involved
    2) Keep the body clean and warm
    3) Cool-down activities may include shaking body parts, massage, stretching, and meditation

Body conditioning

A good body conditioning is also very important to effective table tennis games, training, and preventions of injuries. With proper body conditioning, players can move fast, hit quickly and powerfully, and keep good forms in long games with good endurance. Body conditioning is even essential to the appearance of table tennis players. Table tennis players usually use the paddle-hand to hit the ball, and then it is common that table tennis players are stronger and have more muscles on the paddle-arm but weak on the other arm. Body conditioning certainly helps keep two arms in good balance.

Body conditioning for table tennis player usually include muscle strength especially explosive power, endurance, speed, and agility. Muscle strength can be developed through weight lifting activities. Endurance can be improved through lightweight weight lifting, long distance running, and long time skills training and games. Agility can be enhanced through activities involving quick change of motions and directions. Speed in table can mean footwork speed and hitting speed. The movement speed can be improved through lightweight weight lifting, short distance running, and zigzag ways of running. The hitting speed can be enhanced through increasing the explosive power (the shoulder, arms, and wrist), and efficiency of swing motion, and the transition of movements.

Prevention of injuries in table tennis

Playing table tennis can benefit people in many ways, but there are some risks of injuries involved in this sport, just like any other sport. Almost all professional table tennis players have injuries of different kinds. Although table tennis is relatively safe since there is no body contact as well as less use of maximum force in practice and in games, some people still have the chance of injuries that reduce the benefits of playing the game. Based on research and practical observation, there are a certain typcs of injuries occurred often in table tennis. To prevent these injuries and problems, experts suggest the following guidelines:

1. Health concerns

    1) Consult your physician if you have any physical problems
    2) Consult the instructor or coach if you have any physical problems
    3) Do not play hard when you are ill or injured

2. Environment

    1) Clean up your play area
    2) Beware of what is going on around you
    3) Keep away from other tables, bumping into people or table cause injuries

3. Warm-up

    1) At least 5-8 minutes warm-up before practice or play
    2) Warm-up should include four parts:
        a. run or jump to raise heartbeat and warm muscles
        b. stretch muscles
        c. rotate joints
        d. footwork and swinging

4. Concentration

    1) Focus on your practice or play
    2) Avoid chatting when practicing or playing

5. Equipment and facility

    1) Check the table
    2) Check the surrounding

6. Dress

    1) Wear sportswear.
    2) Wear sport shoes.

Injuries and treatment

1. Relationship of table tennis and injuries

    1) Table tennis can cause injuries
    2) Table tennis can make injuries worse
    3) Table tennis can help prevent injuries
    4) Table tennis can help rehabilitation from injuries
    5) Table tennis *cannot* cure injuries

2. How injuries occur in table tennis

    1) Previous problems
    2) Poor warm-up
    3) Perform techniques incorrectly
    4) Go beyond body limit
    5) Too much repeated movements
    6) Carelessness
    7) Accidents
    8) Quick but jerky motions

3. Potential injuries in table tennis

    1) Sprained or strained wrist
    2) Tennis elbow
    3) Strained or sprained shoulder
    4) Strained neck muscle
    5) Strained upper-back or lower-back muscles
    6) Stained hip and thigh muscles
    7) Sprained knee ligament
    8) Sprained or strained ankle

9) Injured tendon
10) Bump into the table

4. Treatment of injuries

There two styles of medicine people can go for therapies on sport injuries. One is Western style and another is Easter style. Each style has its own pros and cons. The therapeutic techniques used by both styles are listed below.

1) Immediate treatment: Rest
Ice
Seeing doctor
2) Therapy: A. Western: Ice
Heat and cold combination
Aspirin
Compression
Cortisone
Electrical stimulus
Stretching
Exercise
B. Eastern: Heat
Therapeutic massage
Acupuncture
Internal and/or external use of herbs
Chi Gong
Electrical stimulus

C. Comparison: The Western and Eastern medicines both work on sport injuries but are different on their philosophy, major functions, and treatment techniques. In the Western medicine, the procedures of treating injuries are strict and follow a certain process. The Eastern medicine also follows common procedures but sometime adjust by the individual doctors based on their specialties. The Western medicine treats people like a car and only fixes the broken part while the Eastern medicine treats people in a holistic view and tries to treat the roots of the problem. The Western medicine tends to use some drugs to stop the pain from injuries. The pain might be stopped at the brain but the injury is still there but you do not feel it. The Eastern medicine tends to use herbs to stop the pain by speeding up the recovering process. The Western medicine is great at treating the severe injuries such as broken knees by using surgeries and modern technology while the Eastern medicine works very effectively at treating small everyday injuries such as twisted ankle or pulled muscles using acupuncture, therapeutic massage and herbs.

Review questions

1. Will the brand of equipment make significant different to amateur players?
2. What is the difference between pimpled and reverse pimpled paddles?
3. What kind of player use pimple paddles or reverse pimple paddles?
4. What kinds of players tend to use long or
5. What activities should be included in warm-up?
6. What is the function of stretching in warm-up?
7. What is the benefit of rotating joints in warm-up?
8. What is the function of running in warm-up?
9. What are the common ways of cool-down?
10. What is the importance of speed to table tennis players?
11. How do you develop agility for table tennis players?
12. What should you do before participating in table tennis training if you have physical problems?
13. What environment factors may cause injuries in table tennis?
14. What is the relationship between table tennis and injuries?
15. What are the common injuries in table tennis
16. What are the major strategies for preventing injuries in table tennis?
17. What are the major differences between Western and Eastern medicines on their philosophies, functions, and techniques?

Chapter 4

Basics

This chapter mainly introduces basic elements for table tennis skills. These basic elements are important for learning and training of skills. Included are basic stances for serving and receiving, grips, paddle motions for different shots and serves, and footwork.

Ready stance

Like any other sport, a ready stance is essential to movement and skills. The basic stances include serving stances and receiving stance. Photo 4.1a and 4.1b show the basic serving stance for forehand and backhand serves. Photo 4.2a, 4.2b, and 4.2c show the basic receiving stances from front and side views.

1. Basic serving stance (Photo 4.1)

4.1a forehand serving stance   4.1b backhand serving stance

   A. *Performance-forehand* (Photo 4.1a):
      a. one foot away from the table
      b. left foot slightly forward, weight on right foot
      c. left-hand holds the ball at right-front of body
      d. right-hand holds the paddle at right-front of body

   B. *Performance-backhand* (Photo 4.1b):
      a. one foot away from the table
      b. right foot slightly forward, weight on left foot
      c. left-hand holds the ball at left-front of body
      d. right-hand holds the paddle at left-front of body

2. Basic returning stance (Photo 4.2)

4.2a front view of stance   4.2b side view of stance   4.2c over view

Performance:
      a. feet apart shoulder-wide, weight in the middle
      b. knees bent slightly, heels up slightly
      c. the paddle-arm bent naturally with the paddle in front of belly
      d. watch the ball

Basic grips

There are two types of grips in table tennis. One is the "Tennis Grip". The player using this kind of grip holds the paddle in the way similar to the grip for tennis slice shots. The second is "Pen-hold Grip". The player using this kind of grip holds the racket similar to that of holding a pen.

1. The tennis grip (Photo 4.3)

This grip used to be popular among the European players but it is the mostly used grip in the world. This type of grip allows for strong forehand and backhand shots. This grip is also better for loop style and slice style players.

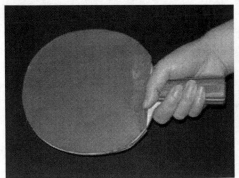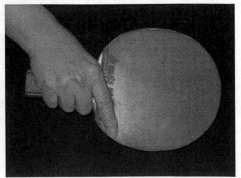

4.3a tennis grip (front view)   4.3b tennis grip (back view)

Performance:
  a. hold the paddle like shaking hands with someone
  b. the thumb is in front and the index finger is at the back
  c. hold the paddle loosely
  d.

2. The traditional pen-grip (Photo 4.4)

This grip is usually used by Asian players, especially Chinese players. This type of grip allows for quick shots, especially for close table style players. But backhand shots from this grip are usually weak since it cannot reach as far on the backhand side, especially for loop and slice shots and off-the-table shots. Although this grip is much less used in the last 10 years, a Korean player used it in 2004 Olympic men's single game and took the champion.

4.4a traditional pen grip (front view) 4.4b traditional pen grip (back view)

Performance:
  a. hold the paddle like holding a pen in the traditional way
  b. both the thumb and the index finger are in front
  c. hold the paddle loosely

3. The new pen-grip (Photo 4.5)

A trend of the pen grip is to imitate the tennis grip style and players using this new style use the back of the paddle to smash, loop, and slice. It is similar to the backhand technique of tennis grip players but still keep the advantage of the traditional style. A Chinese player using this technique won a world championship and another young Chinese player defeated many top players in the 2003 World Championship Games. In 2004 Athens Olympic, a Chinese player took the second place in men's single.

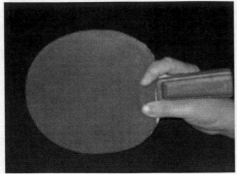
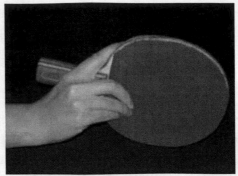

4.5a new pen grip (front view)   4.5b new pen grip (back view)

Performance:
    a. hold the paddle like holding a pen in the traditional way
    b. both the thumb and the index finger are in front, but the index finger is more straight and the thumb press down more

Paddle motion and ball flight directions

The direction and pathway of a serve or a shot depends on how the paddle contacts the ball. There are several ways the paddle contacts the ball and different contacts create different flight patterns of the ball. The contacts include flat, topspin, backspin, and sidespin motions.

1. Flat

In this motion, the paddle directly hits the back of the ball perpendicularly forward, upward or downward. The ball then travels straight forward in flat serves or shots (drive shots), or travels upward in lob shots, or goes down in smash or snap shots accordingly. The direction of a flat motion is showed in Figure 4.1 from a side view.

Figure 4.1 flat flight

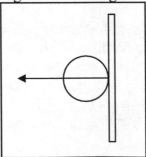

2. Topspin

In this motion, the paddle hits (half hit and half scratch) the top-back of the ball with an upward scratching motion. The ball then travels forward with an upward spin in loop

28

shots. Then the ball bounces up forward with a fast upward spin motion. The direction of topspin is showed in Figure 4.2 from a side view.

Figure 4.2 topspin

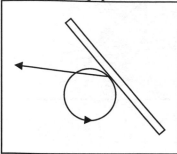

3. Back spin

In this motion, the paddle hits (half hit and half scratch) low on the back of the ball with a downward scratching motion. The ball then travels forward with a backward spin in slice and chop shots and serves. Then the ball bounces up low and slows down with a backspin motion. If the paddle hits the ball fast, it will be a long slice serve or shot. If the paddle hits the ball slowly, then it will be a short and low chop serve or shot. The direction of a backspin is showed in Figure 4.3 from a side view.

Figure 4.3 backspin

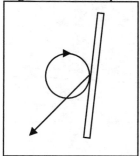

4. Left side spin

In this motion, the paddle hits (half hit and half scratch) the left side of the back of the ball with a sideways scratching motion. The ball then travels forward with a left spin in sidespin serves and shots. If the paddle hits the left side of the back of the ball, then it will be a left side backspin serve or shot. If the paddle hits the top left side of the ball, then it will be a left side topspin serve or shot. Then the ball bounces up sideway toward opponent's left side on opponent's table. The direction of a left spin is showed in Figure 4.4 from a top view.

Figure 4.4 left side spin (top view)

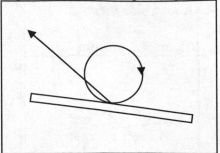

5. Right side spin

In this motion, the paddle hits (half hitting and half scratching) the right of the back of the ball with a sideways scratching motion. The ball then travels forward with a right spin in sidespin serves and shots. If the paddle hits the right side-back of the ball, then it will be a right side-back spin serve or shot. If the paddle hits the right side-top of the ball, then it will be a right side topspin serve or shot. Then the ball bounces up sideway toward opponent's right side on opponent's table. The direction of a right spin is showed in Figure 4.5 from a top view.

Figure 4.5 right side spin (top view)

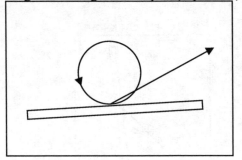

6. Flat and top combination

In this motion, the paddle hits the back of the ball with a lifting motion. The ball then travels forward with an upward arch in flat, lifting, or loop shots. Then the ball bounces up forward with an upward spin motion. Actually this motion is used in most flat, lifting, and upward loop shots since it not only provides an upward arch on the flight of the ball to make it easy to go over the net and come down fast before it gets too long, but also allows more power and speed. The direction of a flat and topspin is showed in Figure 4.6 from a side view.

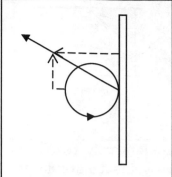

Figure 4.6 flat and topspin

Footwork

Footwork is very important in table tennis. To make effective shots, a player has to position him/herself before hitting the ball. There are several types of footwork.

1. Single Step

Features:
- It is quick and simple in a small range
- It is good for the shots close to the body

A. To right-front (Figure 4.7)

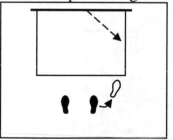

4.7 one step to the right-front

a. left foot pivots to right
b. right foot moves to right-front

B. To Left-front (Figure 4.8)

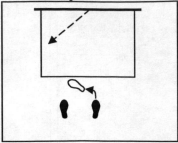

4.8 one step to left-front

a. left foot pivot to left
b. right foot moves to left-front

C. To Right-back (Figure 4.9)

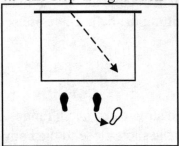

4.9 one step to right-back

a. left foot pivots to right
b. right foot moves to right-back

D. To Left-back (Figure 4.10)

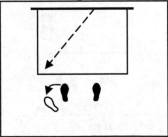

4.10 one step to left-back

a. right foot pivots to left
b. left foot moves to left-back

2. Stride Step

Features:
- It is quick
- It can reach far
- But it is difficult to use continuously

A. Stride steps to right (Figure 4.11)

4.11 stride to right

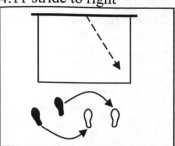

a. left foot pushes and right foot moves to right
b. left foot follows up

B. Stride steps to left (Figure 4.12)

4.12 stride to left

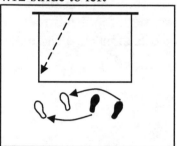

a. right foot pushes and left foot moves to left
b. right foot follows up

3. Jumping Step

Features:
- It can reach far
- It shifts gravity fast
- It lands with same stance and can repeat continuously
- It is good for getting far shots

A. Jump to right (Figure 4.13)

4.13 jump to right

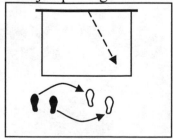

a. left foot pushes
b. both feet take off toward right
c. left foot lands first then right foot
d. keep balance and ready to hit

B. Jump to left (Figure 4.14)

4.14 jump to left

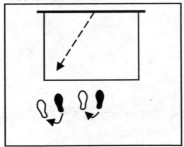

a. right foot pushes
b. both feet take off toward left
c. right foot lands first then left foot
d. keep balance and ready to hit

4. Slide Step (Figure 4.15)

Features:
- It can reach relatively far
- The central gravity is stable when moving

4.15 slide to left

a. similar to the jumping step
b. the right foot moves toward left foot first
c. the left foot moves out
d. reverse the process if moving toward right

5. Pivot steps

A. One step (Figure 4.16)

Features:
- It is used only when using forehand to return backhand shots
- it is used when the ball coming to the body

4.16 pivot one step

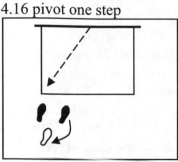

a. left foot pivots clockwise
b. right foot steps back clockwise
c. body turns to right
d. ready to hit

B. Pivot two steps (Figure 4.17)

Features:
- It is used only when using forehand to hit backhand shots
- It is used when the ball coming to the far left

4.17 pivot two steps

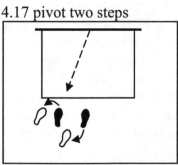

a. left foot steps to left and pivots to right
b. body turns to right
c. right foot step back clockwise

Review questions

1. What is the major difference between forehand and backhand serve stances?
2. Why it is important to maintain a proper stance in practice and games?
3. What are the main characteristics of the tennis grip?
4. What are the main characteristics of the traditional and new pen grips?
5. Which serves or shots use a flat motion?
6. Which serves or shots use a backspin motion?
7. Which serves or shots use a topspin motion?
8. Which serves or shots use the combination motions?

Chapter 5

Flat services and returns

Chapter 5-8 will introduce different services, applications, and returns in table tennis. Services in table tennis can be classified into several types. Based on the positions, there are forehand serves, backhand serves, pivot serves, and squat serves. Based on the toss, there are high-toss serves and low-toss serves. Based on the flight of the ball, there are flat serves and spin serves. Based on the styles, there are spin-oriented serves, speed-oriented serves, and placement-oriented serves. In this chapter, several basic serves will be introduced. For each serve, the tennis-grip serve will be introduced first, and then the pen-grip serves. Since most techniques for both grips are similar, there is not additional explanation for pen-grip serves except that skill is different from the tennis-grip. The letters a, b, c will be used for each sequential movement for tennis-grip photos and capital letters A, B, C will be used for each sequential movement for pen-grip photos of the same serve. Each serve will be introduced in four steps: forehand, backhand, applications, and returns.

This chapter will introduce flat services. Flat serves are fast and travel long toward the baseline. Players often use flat serves to catch opponent off-guard, catch open spots (the corners) or weak spots (such as opponent's body), force weak returns, or force opponent away from the table. The flat serve is also the basic serve in table tennis and other serves can be learned easily after learning the flat serve. Players can return flat serves by using flat shots, block, or loop shots. The paddle motion of flat serves is demonstrated in Chapter 4 (Figure 4.1) and the pathway is showed in Figure 5.1.

Flat serves work better when combined with backspin serves in terms of confusing the opponent's judgment. If the receiver cannot identify which serve (flat or backspin) the server is using, he or she may return with a technique that is not proper for a flat serve, and make mistakes or give weak returns. If the receiver returns a flat serve with a backspin shot, the ball will go high and be smashed easily. The ball will get down to the net if the receiver returns backspin serves with flat shots.

Flat Services

Features:
- It is the base for other serves
- It has no spin or very little spin
- It travels fast and long

Paddle motion and ball pathway (Figure 10.1)

5.1 flat serve

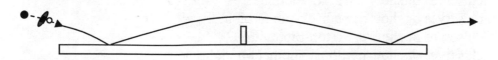

1. Forehand Flat Serve (Photo 5.1)

Preparation:
  a. one foot away from the table (5.1a)
  b. left foot slightly forward, weight on right foot
  c. left hand holds the ball at right-front of body
  d. right hand holds the paddle at right-front of body

Movements:
  a. toss the ball up and right-hand back swing (5.1b)
  b. right hand swings to left-front (5.1c)
  c. hit the ball down-forward at the net level (5.1d and 5.1e)
  d. follow through and shift weight to left foot (5.1f)

A. Tennis-grip

5.1a ready stance

5.1b toss and back swing

5.1c forward swing

5.1d contact

5.1e hit down-forward

5.1f follow through

B. Pen-grip

5.1A ready stance

5.1B toss and back swing

5.1C forward swing

5.1D contact

5.1E hit down-forward

5.1F follow through

2. Backhand Flat Serve (Photo 5.2)

Preparation:
- a. one foot away from the table (5.2a)
- b. right foot slightly forward, weight on left foot
- c. left hand holds the ball at left-front of body
- d. right hand holds the paddle at left-front of body

Movements:
- a. toss the ball up and right hand back swing to left-back (5.2b)
- b. right hand swings to right-front (5.2c)
- c. hit the ball down-forward at the net level (5.2d and 5.2e)
- d. follow through and shift weight to right foot (5.2f)

A. Tennis-grip

5.2a ready stance

5.2b toss and back swing

5.2c forward swing

5.2d contact

5.2e hit down-forward

5.2f follow through

B. Pen-grip

5.2A ready stance

5.2B toss and back swing

5.2C forward swing

5.2D contact

5.2E hit down-forward

5.2F follow through

Applications of the flat serve

a. Serve fast to catch opponent off guard
b. Use fast forehand and backhand serves to confuse the opponent
c. Serve fast to all four corners and to the opponent's body
d. Combine flat serve with spin serves to confuse opponent
e. Change speed and placement to confuse opponent

Return flat serves

a. Smash back if the serve is high
b. Block back if the serve is too fast
c. Use flat shots to return
d. Avoid using slice shots to return
e. Return to opponent's weak spots

Review questions

1. What is the function of flat serves?
2. What are the proper techniques to return flat serves?
3. What will happen when returning flat serves with backspin shots?
4. What are serving strategies for using flat serves?

Chapter 6

Backspin (slice) services and returns

This chapter will introduce backspin serves, returns, and applications. Backspin serves can travel relatively fast, but can also go slowly. These serves can travel long toward the baseline or fall short just over the net. Backspin serves have more flexibility in applications. Players often use backspin serves to keep serves low and give the opponent less chance to attack, especially if the opponent cannot return backspin serves well. Techniques of returning backspin serves include backspin (slice) shots, lifting shots, and loop shots. The paddle motion of backspin serves is demonstrated in Chapter 4 (Figure 4.3) and the pathway is showed in Figure 6.2.

Backspin serves work better when combined with flat serves to confuse opponent and ruin his/her judgment in order to force mistakes or weak returns. If the receiver returns a flat serve with a backspin shot, the ball will get up high and be smashed easily. On the other hand, however, the ball will get down to the net then the ball will get down to the net if the receiver returns a backspin serve with a flat shot. The motions of making backspin serves and flat serves should be identical so that opponent cannot identify which one the server is using. However, making a flat serve and a backspin serve usually sounds different when the paddle hits the ball. To address this problem, professional players tend to stomp the floor to cover the sound.

Backspin (slice) services

Features:
- It is easy to control the ball
- The ball bounces low and hard to attack back
- It confuses opponent when combined with flat serve

Paddle motion and ball flight pathway (Figure 6.1)

6.1 back spin serve

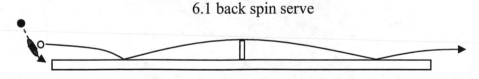

1. Forehand backspin serve (Photo 6.1)

Preparation:
   a. one foot away from the table (6.1a)
   b. left foot slightly forward, weight on right foot
   c. left hand holds the ball at right-front of body
   d. right hand holds the paddle at right-front of body

Movements:
    a. toss the ball up and right hand back swing (6.1b)
    b. right hand swings to down-left with paddle tilt (6.1c)
    c. hit the ball at the net level with a slice motion (6.1d and 6.1e)
    d. follow through and shift weight to left-foot (6.1e and 6.1f)

A. Tennis-grip

6.1a ready stance

6.1b toss and back swing

6.1c forward swing and contact

6.1d slice down-forward

6.1e follow through

B. Pen-grip

6.1A ready stance

6.1B toss and back swing

6.1C forward swing

6.1D contact

6.1E slice down-forward

6.1F follow through

2. Backhand backspin serve (Photo 6.2)

Preparation:
- a. one foot away from the table (6.2a)
- b. right foot slightly forward, weight on left foot
- c. left hand holds the ball at left-front of body
- d. right hand holds the paddle at left-front of body

Movements:
- a. toss the ball up and right hand back swing to left-back (6.2b)
- b. right hand swings to downright with paddle tilt (6.2c)
- c. hit the ball at the net level with a slice motion (6.2d and 6.2e)
- d. shift weight to right foot (6.2e and 6.2f)

6.2a ready stance

6.2b toss and back swing

6.2c forward swing and contact

6.2d slice down-forward

6.2e follow through

B. Pen-grip

6.2A ready stance

6.2B toss and back swing

6.2C forward swing

6.2D contact

6.2E slice down-forward

6.2F follow through

Applications of backspin serve

a. Keep the ball very low
b. Serve to all four lines and two corners and to the opponent's body
c. Change speed to confuse opponent
d. Serve long and serve short to confuse opponent
e. Use a short backspin serve to prevent opponent's attacking shots
f.. Combine with flat serves to catch opponent off guard

Return backspin serves

a. Chop or slice back to keep the return low and safe
b. Lift up and be ready to attack next time whenever there is a chance
c. Use loop shots to attack aggressively

Review questions

1. What is the function of backspin serves?
2. What are the proper techniques to return flat serves?
3. How does a backspin serve work?
4. What will happen when returning slice serves with flat shots?
5. What are serving strategies for using slice serves?

Chapter 7

Side-back spin services and returns

This chapter will introduce side-back spin serves, applications, and returns. Side-back spin serves can travel relatively fast but its main characteristic is to create a side-back spin motion to make the ball going outward to left or right and still remain low. The side-back spin serves usually makes opponent less aggressive since it is low and cannot be smashes easily, and at the same time confuse the opponent on which way to spin back. If they do not use correct spin shots when returning, the ball gets out easily. To return side-backspin serves, people usually use side-backspin shots, lifting shots, loop shots, or off-the-table slice to slice back when the sidespin of the ball is slowing down. The paddle motion of side-backspin serve is demonstrated in Chapter 4 (Figure 4.4 and 4.5) and the pathway is showed in Figure 7.1 and 7.2.

Side-back spin serves works well on receivers who are not familiar with side-backspin serves. Side-back spin serves work better when using left spin and right spin alternatively, and combining with flat and backspin serves to confuse opponent and ruin his/her judgment to force mistakes and weak returns.

Side-back spin services

Features:
- It creates side and backspin and is easy for opponent to hit out
- It is hard for opponent to react fast and return accordingly
- It changes the pathway and is hard to judge and return
- It confuses opponent when combined with other serves

Paddle motion and ball flight pathway-Right Spin (Figur7.1)

7.1 right spin serves

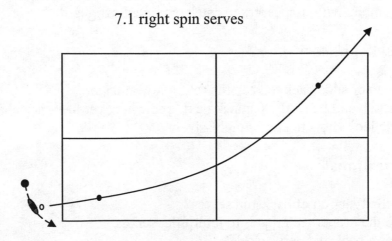

Paddle motion and ball flight pathway-Left Spin (Figure7.2)

46

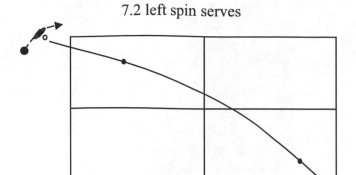

7.2 left spin serves

1. Forehand side-back spin serve—left spin (Photo 7.1)

Preparation:

       a. one foot away from the table

       b. left foot slightly forward, weight on right foot (7.1a)

       c. left hand holds the ball at right-front of body

       d. right hand holds the paddle at right-front of body

Movements:

       a. toss the ball up and right-hand back swing (7.1b)

       b. right-hand swings to down-left with paddle tilt sideways (7.1c)

       c. hit the ball at the net level with a down-side slice motion (7.1d)

       d. wrist continuously snap to create a back-side spin motion (7.1e)

A. Tennis-grip

7.1a ready stance

7.1b toss and back swing

7.1c forward swing and contact

7.1d slice down-side

7.1e follow through

B. Pen-grip

7.1A ready stance

7.1B toss and back swing

7.1C forward swing

7.1D contact with a slice motion

7.1E slice down-side

7.1F follow through

2. Backhand side-back spin serve-right spin (Photo 7.2)

Preparation:
      a. one foot away from the table (7.2a)
      b. right foot slightly forward, weight on left foot
      c. left hand holds the ball at left-front of body
      d. right hand holds the paddle at left-front of body

Movements:
      a. toss the ball up and right hand back swing (7.2 b)
      b. right hand swings to downright with paddle tilt sideways (7.2c)
      c. hit the ball at the net level with a down-side slice motion (7.2d and 7.2e)
      d. wrist snaps down-side to create a side/back spin motion (7.2e and 7.2f)

A. Tennis-grip

7.2a ready stance   7.2b toss and back swing

7.2c forward swing and contact   7.2d slice down-side

7.2e follow through

2-B. Pen-grip

7.2A ready stance

7.2B toss and back swing

7.2C forward swing and contact

7.2D slice down-side

7.2E continue to slice

7.2F follow through

Applications of side-back spin serve

    a. keep the ball very low
    b. change directions to serve to all four corners
    c. change speed to confuse opponent
    d. serve long and short to confuse the opponent
    e. use both forehand and backhand serves to confuse the opponent
    f. combine flat and slice serves to confuse opponent

Return side-back spin serves

      a. use quick spin block
      b. side-back spin back
      c. slice back
      d. wait and return with off-the-table shots
      e. use lift or loop shots

Review questions

1. What is the function of side-back spin serves?
2. What are the proper techniques to return side-back spin serves?
3. How does a side-back spin serve work?
4. What will happen when returning side-back serves with flat shots?
5. What are serving strategies for using side-back serves?

Chapter 8

Side-top spin services and returns

This chapter will introduce side-top spin serves, returns, and applications. Side-top spin serves can travel fast and it also creates a side-top spin motion to make the ball going far outward to left and right and still remain the speed. The side-top spin serves usually catch opponent off-guard and keep opponent guessing which way the ball spins, thus make opponent less prepared and less aggressive. If they do not use correct spin shots when returning the serve, the ball gets out easily. To return side-top spin serves, people usually use sidespin blocks, smash, loop, or off-the-table slice shots to slice back when the side-top spin motion weakened. The side-top spin serve is aggressive but it can be smashed since it is usually high. The paddle motion of side-backspin serve is demonstrated in Chapter 4 (Figure 4.4 and 4.5) and the pathway is showed in Figure 8.1 and 8.1.

Side-top-spin serves work well to receivers who are not good at returns side-top spin serves, and work better when using left spin and right spin alternatively. When combined with flat and backspin as well as side-back serves, this will further confuse opponent and ruin his/her judgment to force mistakes and weak returns.

Side-top spin services

Features:

- It creates side-top spin and is easy to hit out for opponent
- It is difficult for opponent to react fast and return accordingly
- It changes the pathway and is hard to judge and return
- It confuses opponent when combined with other serves
- It can go very fast and catch opponent off-guard

Paddle motion and ball flight pathway-Right Spin (Figure 8.1)

8.1 right side-top spin

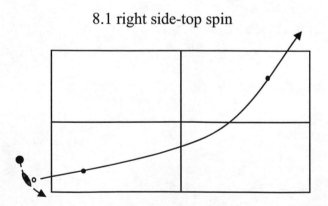

Paddle motion and ball flight pathway-Left Spin (Figure 8.

8.1 left side-top spin

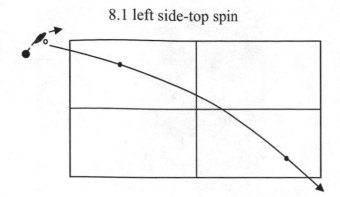

1. Forehand side-top spin serve—left spin (Photo 8.1)

Preparation:
        a. *one* foot away from the table (8.1a)
        b. left foot slightly forward, weight on right foot
        c. left hand holds the ball at right-front of body
        d. right hand holds the paddle at right-front of body

Movements:
        a. toss the ball up and right-hand back swing (8.1b)
        b. right-hand swings to down-left with paddle tilt sideways (8.1c)
        c. hit the ball at the net level with a side slice motion (8.1d and 8.1e)
        d. wrist continuously snaps to create a top/sidespin motion (8.1e and 8.1f)

A. Tennis-grip

8.1a ready stance

8.1b toss and back swing

8.1c forward swing sideways

8.1d slice side-up with a wrist snap

53

8.1e follow through to left-up

B. Pen-grip

8.1A ready stance

8.1B toss and back swing

8.1C forward swing sideways

8.1D slice sideways

8.1E wrist snap up

8.1F follow through to left-up

2. Backhand side-top spin serve--right spin (Photo 8.2)

Preparation:

        a. one foot away from the table (8.2)

        b. right foot slightly forward, weight on left foot

        c. left hand holds the ball at left-front of body

        d. right hand holds the paddle at left-front of body

Movements:

        a. toss the ball up and right hand back swing (8.2b)

        b. right hand swings down-right with paddle tilt sideways (8.2c)

        c. hit the ball at the net level with a side slice motion (8.2d and 8.2e)

        d. wrist continuously snap to create a topspin motion (8.2e and 8.2f)

A. Tennis-grip

8.2a ready stance

8.2b toss and back swing

8.2c forward swing sideways

8.2d slice side-up with a wrist snap

8.1e follow through to right-up

8.2A ready stance

8.2B toss and back swing

8.2C forward swing sideways

8.1D slice sideways

8.1E wrist snap up

8.1F follow through to right-up

Applications of side-top spin serve

    a. Keep the ball fast and spin-up sideways
    b. Serve to all four lines and two corners
    c. Change speed and angles to confuse opponent
    d. Use both forehand and backhand serves to confuse opponent
    e. Combine with back-spin, back-side spin, and flat serves

Return side-top spin serves

      a. Smash back if the serve is high
      b. Quick spin block or push with paddle tilt sideways
      c. Wait and return it off-table with loop or slice
      d. Loop up

Review questions

1.   What are features of side-top spin serves?
2.   What are the proper techniques to return side-back spin serves?
3.   How does a side-top spin serve work?
4.   What are serving strategies for using side-top serves?

Chapter 9

Flat shots

This chapter will introduce different types of flat shots and returns. These shots will be introduced in a format of forehand and backhand, and tennis grip and pen grip. In most shots, the tennis grip and pen-grip are similar and the explanation will be the same unless there are differences.

Close-table flat shots

Close-table flat shots are basic techniques in table tennis. These shots are fast and can be placed at big angles since it is performed at close-table positions. The pathway is short and this gives opponent less time to prepare and return with high quality. Players often use these shots to catch opponent off-guard, and catch open spots (the corners) or weak spots (such as opponent's body). Players can also use these shots to press opponent to play fast and be unprepared for using strong returns (such as loop). All types of players should handle the close-table flat shot not only because it is the basic skill but also it is used often in the actual games. Flat shots can be returned effectively by using flat shots, push, block, or loop shots depending on the situation and your preferred shots or style. The close-table, fast attack style players tend to use this kind of shots. It is not proper to return flat shots with backspin shots since the ball will go high and give your opponent more chances to smash. The paddle motion of flat serves is demonstrated in Chapter 4 (Figure 4.1) and the pathway is showed in Figure 9.1.

Features:
- It is more like the flat serves.
- It has more power and is fast
- It is often used to return flat serves and shots
- It controls placement well and hits bigger angles

Paddle motion and ball flight pathway-Drive (Figure 9.1)

9.1 flat shot (drive) pathway

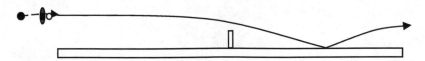

Preparation:
    a. one foot away from the table
    b. flat steps with weight between feet
    c. hold the paddle in front of the body

1. Forehand close-table flat shots (Photo 9.1)

Features:
- It is powerful
- It is fast and gives opponent less time to prepare
- It can hit bigger angles
- It blocks fast serves and shots easily

Movement:

a. from ready stance (9.1a), rotate right shoulder backward while keep the paddle tilt to the table and use a small back swing (9.1b)

b. rotate body to left and swing fast forward, contact the ball at right-front (9.1c)

c. lift up-forward (9.1d)

d. follow through up-left (9.1e)

A. Tennis-grip

9.1a ready stance

9.1b back swing to right

9.1c forward swing and contact

9.1d forward swing with lifting motion

9.1e follow through up-left

9.1A ready stance

9.1B back swing to right

9.1C forward swing and contact

9.1D forward swing with lifting motion

9.1E follow through up-left

2. Backhand close-table flat shots (Photo 9.2-9.4)

Features:
- It is used to deal with flat serves and shots
- It has less power and speed than forehand
- It has more control on the placement
- It can hit wide angles
- It can be very aggressive
- It blocks fast flat serves and shots easily

Movement:

        a. from ready stance (9.2a) rotate left shoulder backward while keep the paddle tilt to the table and use a small back swing (9.2b)

        b. rotate body to right and small swing forwards, contact the ball at left-front (9.2c)

        c. lift up-forward (9.2d)

        d. follow through to right (9.2e)

A. Tennis-grip drive

9.2a ready stance

9.2b back swing to right

9.2c forward swing and contact

9.2d forward swing with lifting motion

9.2e continue to hit forward

9.2f follow through up-left

B. Pen-grip push

Features:
- It is fast
- It has more consistency and makes less mistakes
- It has more control on the placement
- It is, however, lack of power and speed
- It is, however, hard to reach far backhanded
- It blocks fast flat serves and shots easily

Movement:
a. ready stance (9.2A)
b. a small back swing, keep the paddle a little tilt to the table (9.2B)
b. push forward with a little lifting motion with pedal tilt down (9.2C)
c. keep pushing forward (9.2D)
d. follow through forward

9.2A ready stance

9.2B small back swing

9.2C contact in front of body

9.2D push forward

9.2E follow through forward

C. Pen-grip power push

9.3A ready stance

9.3B big back swing

9.3C contact in front of body

9.3D power push forward

9.3E follow through further forward

D. Pen-grip drive

Features:
- It uses the back of paddle and it is similar to the tennis grip
- It has more power than push shot

Movement:
a. from ready stance (9.4A) rotate left shoulder backward while keep the paddle tilt to the table and use a small back swing (9.4B)

b. rotate body to right and swing fast forwards, contact the ball at left-front (9.4C)
c. lift up-forward (9.4D)
d. follow through to right (9.4E and 9.4F)

9.4A ready stance

9.4B small back swing

9.4C contact at left-front

9.4D lift up-forward

9.4E continue to lift up-right

9.4F follow through up-right

Off-table flat shots

Off-table shots are similar to close-table shots except performed away from the table for long shots. These shots can go very fast but the angles are not as big as the close-table shots. Players often use these shots to attack, drive opponent far away from the table and make opponent less aggressive, and return off-table shots. These shots also can be used to press opponent to play fast and force opponent unprepared for using strong returns (such as loop). Most players should also handle the off-table flat shots not only because they are the basic skills but also they are used often in the actual games. Off-table flat shots can be returned effectively by using flat shots, block, push, slice, or loop shots. The paddle motion of flat serves is demonstrated in Chapter 4 (Figure 4.1) and the pathway is showed in Figure 9.2.

Features:
- It has more powerful and smashes very hard
- It is used to deal with off-table flat shots and loop shots

Paddle motion and ball flight pathway (Figure 9.2)

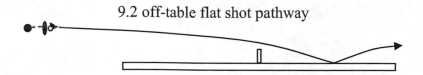

9.2 off-table flat shot pathway

Movement:
a. ready stance (9.5a), rotate to right and use a big back swing, keep the paddle a little tilt to the table (9.5b)
c. rotate left and swing forward-up (9.5c)
d. contact at right-front (9.5d)
d. lift up-forward (9.5e), and follow through up-left (9.5f)

1. Forehand off-table flat shots (Photo 9.5)

A. Tennis-grip

9.5a ready stance   9.5b big back swing

65

9.5c forward swing

9.5d contact with up-forward motion

9.5e lift with full body rotation

9.5f follow through left-up

B. Pen-grip

9.5A ready stance

9.5B big back swing

9.5C forward swing

9.5D contact with up-forward motion

9.5E lift with full body rotation   9.5F follow through left-up

2. Backhand off-table flat shots (Photo 9.6)

Features:

- It is used to deal with flat serves and shots off the table
- The shot can be very fast and aggressive
- It places the ball to corners and drive opponent off the table
- It has more power when returning high shots

Movement:

    a. ready stance (9.6a)

    b. rotate the should back with a back swing motion, keep the paddle tilt to the table (9.6b), pen-grip tilt the back little downward

    c. rotate body and swing to right-up-front (9.6c)

    d. hit the ball with a lifting motion and snap wrist upward (9.6d)

    e. follow through up-right (9.6f)

A. Tennis-grip

9.6a ready stance   9.6b back swing

9.6c forward swing and contact

9.6d hit up-forward

9.6e follow through up-right

B. Pen-grip traditional drive

Features:

- It is used to deal with flat serves and shots and loops
- It has more consistency and more control on the placement
- However, it lacks power and speed
- It is also more difficult to reach far at backhand

Movement:

a. ready stance (9.7A), a big back swing, keep the paddle a little tilt to the table (9.7B)
b. swing forward with a little lifting motion with pedal tilt down (9.7C)
c. contact the ball at left-front with a lifting motion (9.7D)
d. continue to hit forward with pedal tilt down more (9.7E and 9.7F)
e. follow through forward up-right (9.7G)

9.7A ready stance

9.7B big back swing to left

9.7C paddle tilt at forward swing   9.7D contact at left-front

9.7E hit flat forward   9.7F turn paddle face down more

9.7G follow up to up-right

B. Pen-grip (new grip) drive

Features:
- It uses the back of paddle and it is similar to the tennis grip
- It has more power than push shot

Movement:
     a. from ready stance (9.8A) rotate left shoulder backward while keep the paddle tilt to the table and use a small back swing (9.8B)
     b. rotate body to right and swing fast forwards, contact the ball at left-front (9.8C)
     c. lift up-forward (9.8D)
     d. follow through to right (9.8E and 9.8F)

9.8A ready stance

9.8B small back swing

9.8C contact at left-front

9.8D lift up-forward

9.8E continue to lift up-right

9.8F follow through up-right

Smash

Features:

- It is used to kill high shots
- It is very powerful
- It uses forehand most time
- It needs a pivot motion to hit the backhand side shots

Paddle motion and ball flight pathway-Smash (Figure 9.3)

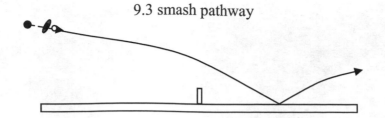

9.3 smash pathway

Movement:

    a. from ready stance (9.9a), rotate right shoulder backward while keep the paddle tilt to the table and use a big back swing (9.9b and 9.9c)

    b. rotate body to left and swing fast forward, contact the ball at right-front (9.9d)

    c. lift up with the paddle on back-top (9.9e)

    d. follow through down-left (9.9f)

A. Tennis grip

9.9a ready stance

9.9b back swing

9.9c continue back swing

9.9d lift up-forward at right-front

71

9.9e. keep paddle tilt downward

9.9f follow through down-right

B. Pen-grip

9.9A ready stance

9.9B back swing

9.9C continue back swing

9.9D lift up-forward at right-front

9.9E. keep paddle tilt downward

9.9F follow through down-right

Applications of the flat shots

a. Hit fast to catch opponent off guard
b. Hit fast to two corners and to the opponent's body
c. Force opponent to play fast with you and change his/her style
d. find every chance to kill opponent's shots

Return flat shots

a. Smash back if the serve is high
b. Block back if the serve is too fast
c. Use flat shots to return
d. Avoid using slice shots to return
e. Return to opponent's weak spots

Review questions

1. What is the advantage of close-table flat shots?
2. How should one return close-table shots effectively?
3. What are differences between close and off-table shots?
4. How to use off-table shots in games?
5. What is the difference between traditional and new pen-grip backhand shots?
6. How to smash a high shot on the backhand side?

Chapter 10

Short shots

This chapter will introduce different types of short shots usually performed above the table and returns. Included are snap shot and lift shots. These shots will be introduced in a format of forehand and backhand, and tennis grip and pen grip. In most shots, the tennis grip and pen-grip are similar and the explanation will be similar unless there are differences.

Snap shots

The snap shot is similar to close-table shots and it is used often when opponent's shot is short and high over the table and close to the net. Players can perform this shot by using a forearm and wrist motion, and it is more like a quick smash with small motions. People often catch the chance to use snap shots while they are doing chop rallies. The snap shot is very difficult to return since it is very close and fast and opponent usually has no time to react. The only way to return is to block. The paddle motion of flat serves is demonstrated in Chapter 4 (Figure 4.1) and the pathway is showed in Figure 10.1.

Features:
- It is used to deal with short high shots and serves
- It is fast and hard to react to it

Paddle motion and ball flight pathway (Figure 10.1)

10.1 snap shot pathway

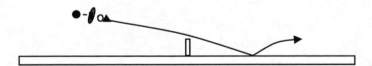

Movement:
    a. ready stance (10.1a), move quickly to the table and use a wrist back swing motion to reach to the ball (10.1b)
    b. use small forward swing motion to catch the ball high (10.1c)
    c. use quick wrist motion to lift up and hit angles (10.1d)
    d. follow through up-right (10.1e)

1. Forehand snap shot (Photo 10.1)

    A. Tennis-grip

10.1a ready stance

10.1b reach early

10.1c lift up

10.1d continue to lift and hit angles

10.1e follow through up-right

B. Pen-grip

10.1A ready stance

10.1B reach with a small back swing

10.1C lift up

10.1D continue to lift and hit angles

10.1E follow through up-right

2. Backhand snap shot (Photo 10.2)

Movement:

a. ready stance (10.2a), move quickly and use a small wrist swing motion to reach the ball early (10.2b)

b. use small forward swing motion to catch the ball high (10.2c)

c. use quick wrist motion to lift up and hit angles (10.2d)

A. <u>Tennis-grip</u>

10.2a ready stance

10.2b reach the ball early

10.2c lift up at contact   10.2d continue to hit up-forward

10.2e follow through up-right

B. Pen-grip

10.2A reach the ball early   10.2B lift up at contact

10.2C follow through up-right

Short lift shots

The short lifting shot is similar to snap shots except it usually starts lower and has more scratching and lifting motion. These shots allow players to lift the ball over the net when the shot is short and low. Lifting shots can be returned effectively using snap, loop, or chop shots.

Features:
- It is used to deal with very short and low shots and serves
- It can lift the ball over the net

Movement:
a. ready stance (10.3a), reach the ball early with paddle low (10.3b)
b. lift up slightly with top spin motion without back swing (10.3c)
c. continue to lift (10.3d)
d. follow up to bring the ball over the net (10.3e)

1. Forehand lift shot (Photo 10.3a-e)

Tennis-grip

10.3a ready stance

10.3b reach the ball early

10.3c lift up slightly

10.3d continue to lift

10.3e follow through forward

2. Backhand lift shot (Photo 10.3A-E)

<u>Pen-grip</u>

10.3A ready stance

10.3B reach the ball early

10.3C lift up slightly

10.3D continue to lift

10.3F follow through forward

Applications of the short shots

     a. Be aggressive when opponent's serve/shot is high and close to the net
     b. Lift up if the shot is too low or too close to the net
     d. Hit angles to confuse opponent

Return short shots

     a. Snap back if the serve is high
     b. Slice it if it is low and opponent is ready to snap
     c. Hit angles
     d. Return to opponent's weak spots

Review questions

1. What is the function of snap shots?
2. How should one return snap shots effectively?
3. What is the function of short lift shots?
4. How should one return short lift shots effectively?
5. What are differences between snap and lift shots?

Chapter 11

Loop (top spin) shots

This chapter will introduce loop shots, application, and returns. Loop shots are faster and have very strong upward or forward top spin motion. The upward loop shots bounce up high and far as well as fast, and forces opponent to back up from the table and play defensively with weak returns since it is difficult for opponent to aim and smash. The forward loop shots bounce off the table low with a greater speed and give opponent less time to prepare for a good return. Players mainly use loop shots to make the defensive players who use more slices to change their play from their favorite shots to following the loop style and make more mistakes or weak returns. The loop players tend to use this kind of shots to change from defensive play to offensive play. Loop shots can be returned effectively using smash, push, block, loop, or slice shots. The paddle motion of flat serves is demonstrated in Chapter 4 (Figure 4.2 and 4.6) and the pathway is showed in Figure 11.1 and 11.2.

Fast loop

Features:

- It is used effectively to deal with low and backspin shots and serves
- It creates fast top spin at the bounce
- It lifts the ball up and attack immediately
- It can return all serves and shots aggressively

Paddle motion and ball flight pathway (Figure 11.1)

11.1 fast loop shot pathway

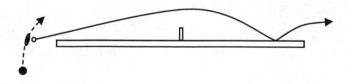

1. Forehand fast loop shot (Photo 11.1)

Movement:
a. ready stance (11.1a), rotate to right and big back swing (11.1b)
b. rotate to left with a sharp forward top spin motion at contact (11.1c)
c. lift the ball up with a strong topspin scratching motion (11.1d)
d. rotate and use full power across the body with paddle tilt down (11.1e)
e. bring the ball up-forward (11.1e), and follow through to left (11.1f)

A. Tennis-grip

11.1a ready stance

11.1b rotate and back swing

11.1c lift with sharp top spin

11.1d scratch the ball with top spin

11.1e full body rotate

11.1f follow through up-left

B. Pen-grip

11.1A ready stance

11.1B rotate and back swing

| 11.1C lift with sharp top spin | 11.1D scratch the ball with top spin |

| 11.1E rotate and spin up | 11.1F follow through |

2. Backhand fast loop shots (Photo 11.2)

Movement:

        a. ready stance (11.2a), rotate to left and big back swing (11.2b)
        b. rotate to right with a sharp forward top spin motion at contact (11.2c)
        c. lift the ball up with a strong topspin scratching motion (11.2d)
        d. rotate and use full power across the body with paddle tilt down (11.2e)
        e. bring the ball up-forward (11.2e), and follow through to right (11.2f)

<u>A. Tennis-grip</u>

| 11.2a ready stance | 11.2b rotate and back swing |

11.2c lift with sharp top spin

11.2d scratch the ball with top spin

11.2e lift up

11.2f follow through up-right

B. Pen-grip

11.2A ready stance

11.2B rotate and back swing

11.2C lift with sharp top spin

11.2D scratch the ball with top spin

11.2E lift up   11.2F follow through up-right

High Loop

Features:

- It is used effectively to deal with low and backspin shots and serves
- It creates very high top spin at the bounce and it is hard to return
- It lifts the ball up fast and attack immediately
- It can return all serves and shots aggressively

Paddle motion and ball flight pathway (Figure 11.2)

11.2 high loop shot pathway

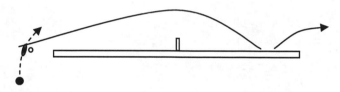

1. Forehand high loop shot (Photo 11.3)

Movement:

a. ready stance (11.3a), rotate to right and big back swing (11.3b)
b. rotate to left with a sharp upward top spin motion at contact (11.3c)
c. lift the ball up with a strong topspin scratching motion (11.3d)
d. rotate and use full power across the body with paddle tilt slightly (11.3e)
e. bring the ball up-forward (11.3e), and follow through to left (11.3f)

<u>A. Tennis-grip</u>

11.3a ready stance

11.3b rotate and back swing

11.3c lift with high top spin motion

11.1d scratch the ball up with top spin

11.3e full body rotate to lift up

11.3f follow through up-left

<u>B. Pen-grip</u>

11.3A ready stance

11.3B rotate and back swing

11.3C lift with high top spin motion 11.1D scratch the ball up with top spin

11.3E full body rotate to bring ball up 11.3F follow through up-left

2. Backhand high loop shot (Photo 11.4)

Movement:

        a. ready stance (11.4a), rotate to left and big back swing (11.4b)
        b. rotate to right with a sharp upward top spin motion at contact (11.4c)
        c. lift the ball up with a strong topspin scratching motion (11.4d)
        d. rotate and use full power across the body with paddle tilt slightly (11.4e)
        e. bring the ball up-forward (11.4e), and follow through to right (11.3F)

A. Tennis-grip

11.4a ready stance 11.4b rotate and back swing

11.4c lift with high top spin motion   11.4d scratch the ball up with top spin

11.4e bring the ball up   11.4f follow through up-right

B. Pen-grip

11.4A ready stance   11.4B rotate and back swing

11.4C lift with high top spin motion   11.4D scratch the ball up with top spin

11.4E bring the ball up 11.4F follow through up-right

Applications of the loop shots

a. To deal with low and backspin shots and serves
b. Lifts the ball up and attack immediately
c. Use more if opponent does not deal with it effectively
d. Change the pace of the game aggressively

Return loop shots

a. Smash back if the loop is high
b. Fast return to opponent's middle
c. Loop back
d. Slice it low
e. Tilt push to cut off (Photo 11.5)

11.5a ready stance 11.5b back swing

11.5c push down-side at early bounce 11.5d tilt down to press the loop down

Review questions

1. What is the function of fast loop shots?
2. What are the features of high loop shots?
3. What is the difference between fast and high loop shots?
2. How should one return loop shots effectively?
3. When should you use loop shots in the games?

Chapter 12

Backspin (slice & chop) shots

Backspin shots are just the opposite of loop in terms of their spin motion. Backspin shots are not powerful or fast, but are more consistent and make fewer mistakes than offensive shots. Furthermore, backspin shots fly with a back spin motion and bounce very low and short, thus give opponent less chance to smash. The defensive style players tend to use slice shots most time in their play but they also use offensive shots whenever a return is high. Players mainly use slice shots to reduce their own mistakes while forcing opponent to have less patience therefore make more mistakes, to make opponent less aggressive, and to force offensive players to change their play from their offensive shots to defensive play. Slice shots can be returned effectively using loop or slice shots. The backspin shots should not be returned with flat shots since the ball usually gets into the net. The paddle motion of flat serves is demonstrated in Chapter 4 (Figure 4.3) and the pathway is shown in Figure 12.1.

Slice shots

Features:
- It is used to deal with low, slice, and loop shots
- It man make opponent less aggressive
- It makes opponent impatient
- It can create chances for fast attacks
- It is consistent and force the opponent to make mistakes

Paddle motion and ball flight pathway (Figure12.1)

12.1 slice shot pathway

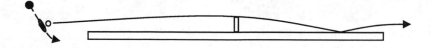

Movement:
a. ready stance (12.1a), use a big back swing motion (12.1b)
b. tilt the paddle a little upward when hitting the ball (12.1c)
c. slice the ball forward to make it spin backward and fly low (12.1d)
d. continue to slice forward (12.1e) and follow through to left (12.1f)

1. Forehand off-table slice shot (Photo 12.1)

A. Tennis-grip

12.1a ready stance

12.1b big back swing

12.1c forward swing with paddle tilt

12.1d slice the low-back of the ball

12.1e continue to slice forward

12.1f follow through

<u>B. Pen-grip</u>

12.1A ready stance

12.1B big back swing

12.1C forward swing with paddle tilt   12.1D slice the low-back of the ball

12.1E continue to slice forward   12.1F follow through down-forward

12.1f follow through to up-right

2. Backhand off-table slice shot (Photo 12.2)

A. Tennis-grip

Movement:

  a. ready stance (12.2a), use a big back swing motion (12.2b)
  b. tilt the paddle a little upward when hitting the ball (12.2c)
  c. slice the ball forward to make it spin backward and fly low (12.2d)
  d. continue to slice forward (12.2e) and follow through to left (12.2f)

12.2a ready stance

12.2b big back swing

12.2c forward swing with paddle tilt

12.2d slice the low-back of the ball

12.2e continue to slice forward

12.2f follow through

B. Pen-grip

Movement:
     a. change the grip and only keep the thumb in front
     a. use a big back swing motion (12.2A)
     b. tilt the paddle a little upward when hitting the ball (12.2B)
     c. slice the ball forward to make it spin backward and fly low (12.2C)
     d. continue to slice forward (12.2D)
     e. follow through down-forward (12.2E) and to up-left (12.2F)

12.2A big back swing

12.1B forward swing with paddle tilt

12.2C slice the low-back of the ball

12.2D continue to slice forward

12.2E follow through down-forward

12.2F follow through to up-right

Chop shots

The chop shot is a slice shot except slice shot is usually long and the chop shot is short. Slice shots are usually performed with the off-table technique and travel far while the chop shot is low and short. The chops usually hit and land close to the net. The chop shot is not as powerful or fast, but it is more consistent and makes fewer mistakes. The chop shot also flies with a backspin motion and bounces very low and short, thus it gives opponent no chance to smash or to be aggressive. Most players often use the chop shot in games to avoid being smashed and to create chances to smash. Players also use chop shots to reduce their own mistakes while force opponent to make opponent less patience and consequently make more mistakes, to make the opponent less aggressive, and to force offensive players to change their play style to defensive play. Chop shots can be returned effectively using chops or quick lift and snap shots. The paddle motion of flat serves is demonstrated in Chapter 4 (Figure 4.3) and the pathway is showed in Figure 12.2.

Features:

- It is used to deal with low and shot backspin shots and serves
- It can make the opponent less aggressive
- It can create chances for attacks and it is consistent and has fewer risks

Paddle motion and ball flight pathway (Figure12.2)

12.2 chop shot pathway

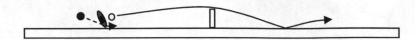

Movement:

a. ready stance (12.3a), reach forward and use small backs wing motion (12.3b)
b. tilt the paddle back when hitting the ball at it low-back(12.3c)
c. slightly slice forward to make the shot short and low (12.3d)
d. follow through forward-sideways

1. Forehand chop shot (Photo 12.3)

A. Tennis-grip

12.3a ready stance   12.3b reach early and small back swing

12.3c slice the low-back of the ball   12.3d slice forward

12.3e follow through

B. Pen-grip

12.3A ready stance   12.3B reach early and small back swing

12.3C slice the low-back of the ball   12.3D slice forward

97

12.3E follow through

2. Backhand chop shot (Photo 12.4)

A. Tennis-grip

12.4a ready stance

12.4b reach early and small back swing

12.4c slice the low-back of the ball

12.4d slice forward

12.4e follow through

B. Pen-grip

12.4A ready stance

12.4B reach early and small back swing

12.4C slice the low-back of the ball

12.4D slice forward

12.4E follow through forward

12.4F follow through to right

Snap chop

The snap chop is a very short chop shot and tries to keep the chop very low and shot so that opponent has no chance to attack at all. This shot has no back swing and the forward swing motion is very small. Snap chop can be returned effectively using snap chops or quick lift and snap shots. The paddle motion of flat serves is demonstrated in Chapter 4 (Figure 4.3) and the pathway is showed in Figure 12.5.

Features:
- It is used to deal with very low and shot chop shots and serves
- It create extremely short and low shots and make the opponent much less aggressive
- It can create chances for attacks
- It is consistent and has fewer risks

Paddle motion and ball flight pathway (Figure12.3)

12.3 snap chop pathway

Movement:
a. ready stance (12.5a), reach forward without backswing motion (12.3b)
b. tilt the paddle back when hitting the ball at it low-back(12.5c)
c. slightly slice forward with wrist motion (12.5d)
d. follow through forward-sideways (12.5e)

1. Forehand snap chop (Photo 12.5)

A. Tennis-grip

12.5a ready stance   12.5b reach early without backswing

12.5c chop with wrist motion

12.5d chop through the back of the ball

12.5e follow through

B. Pen-grip

12.5A ready stance

12.5B reach early without backswing

12.5C chop with wrist motion

12.5D chop through the back of the ball

12.5E follow through

1. Forehand snap chop (Photo 12.6)

A. Tennis-grip

12.6a ready stance

12.6b reach early without backswing

12.6c chop with wrist motion

12.6d chop through the back of the ball

12.6e follow through

B. Pen-grip

12.6A ready stance

12.6B reach early without backswing

12.6C chop with wrist motion

12.6D chop through the back of the ball

12.6E follow through

Applications of the backspin shots

    a.   Return low and backspin shots and serves
    b.   Keep the shots low and short to avoid attacks
    c.   Reduce mistakes and force opponent to slow down or make mistakes
    d.   Change the angles and length of the backspin
    e.   Attack when there is an opportunity

Return backspin shots

    a. Slice or chop back
    b. Loop it up and attack

Review questions

1. What is the function of backspin shots?
2. What is the difference between slice and chop, and between chop and snap chop?
3. How can you use backspin shots in the game effectively?
4. How to return slices and chops?

Chapter 13

Combination shots

It is very difficult to score with one shot in table tennis games. Very often players have to combine several skills together with strategic purposes to win an inning. Players usually develop their own style of combinations and based these combinations establish their unique styles. The following are several common combination skills in table tennis.

Push then pivot attack (Photo 13.1)

Players with the traditional pen-grip use this combination most frequently. It mainly uses the backhand to push the ball for good placement, and then catch any chances to use forehand to smash or loop.

Features:
- It is aggressive at the forehand and backhand sides
- It effectively controls the placements before the attack
- It is consistent and make fewer mistakes

Movement:
a. use backhand push or block first (13.1a)
b. move to backhand side with left shoulder/foot in front and back swing (13.1b), and use forehand to attack (13.1c)

13.1a push

13.1b pivot

13.1c attack

Backhand push then forehand attack (Photo 13.2)

Close-table players with traditional pen-grip are the most frequent users of this combination. It mainly uses the backhand to push the ball for good placement and to defend, then catches chances to attack with forehand smash or loop shots.

Features:
- It is aggressive at the forehand side
- It is defensive but consistent at backhand side
- It makes less mistakes on backhand

Movement:
    a. use backhand push for defense or control placement (13.2a)
    b. use forehand to attack (13.2b)

13.2a backhand push   13.2b forehand attack

Chop, lift, and attack (Photo 13.3)

Generally, offensive players are the most common users of this combination. It mainly uses backhand and forehand chops to make shots short and low, and then catches any chances to lift the ball for the next attack with loop or smash.

Features:
- It uses short chops in rally to create chances for attacks
- It lifts the ball up for offensive shots
- It changes the play from defense to offense

Movement:
    a. use backhand chop continuously (13.3a)
    b. lift the ball when the shot is long and low (13.3b)
    c. smash when chance comes (13.3c)

13.3a chops continuously

13.3b lift with a high loop

13.3c attack with smash

Chop and snap (Photo 13.4)

All players use this combination. It mainly uses short and low chops to prevent any smashes from an opponent and catches any chances to snap or smash if opponent's return is high.

Features:
- It uses short chops in rally to reduce mistakes
- It attacks with snap shots when the return is high
- It is safe but can be aggressive when there is a chance

Movement:
a. use chops continuously with forehand or backhand (13.4a)
b. attack whenever the shot is high with forehand or backhand (13.4b)

13.4a chops or snap chops in rally   13.4b snap it at high returns

Lift and attack (Photo 13.5)

Mostly offensive players use this combination. It is mainly use high loop shots to lift up low slices, and then catches any chances to attack with fast loops or smashes.

Features:
- It is used to deal with slice players
- It forces opponent to change the pace and height of the shots

Movement:
  a. lift the ball up with high loops (13.5a)
  b. use flat drive, smash, or fast loop shots to attack (13.5b)

13.5a lift with high loop   13.5b attack with forehand drive

Slice and attack (Photo 13.6)

Generally defensive players use this combination with a tennis-grip. It mainly uses slice shots to keep the ball low and keep opponent away from the table so that opponent can not be aggressive. Then whenever there is opportunity, the player should attack back immediately with flat shots, smashes, or loop shots.

Features:
- It is mainly used by slice type players
- It can makes opponent less aggressive

- It looks for chances to attack back
- It is very consistent and make less mistakes

Movement:

    a. use low slice shots continuously (13.6a)

    b. attack back with smashes, loops, or flat shots when there is a chance (13.6b)

13.6a slices in rally   13.6b attach with fast loop

Review questions

1. What kind of players tends to use push and pivot combinations?
2. What is the advantage of the backhand push and forehand attack?
3. When is the combination chop-lift-attack used?
4. How do players use chop-snap combination?
5. What kind of players tends to use lift-attack combination?
6. What kind of players tends to use slice and attack combinations?

Chapter 14

Practice guidelines and drills

This chapter will introduce guidelines and drills for serves, returning serves, and shots. The guidelines and drills are basic for all players. Player should choose drills based on their individual needs and combine these drills to make their individual practice creative.

Practice guidelines and drills for services

Learning the basic serves is only the first step in learning table tennis and there is a long way between learning the serves and using the serves in games. Step-by-step practice and drills designed based on the application features in various game situations of table tennis need to be followed so that students can move from learning the basic serves into applying them in games effectively. The following guidelines provide these sequential steps so instructors and students can adopt or create drills to improve skills and their applications. However, this may not be the model for everyone. People can combine two steps together, or skip some steps, or reverse these step based on the individual needs of players.

Step 1. List all serves to be practiced

1. Flat serves
2. Backspin (slice) serves
3. Left back-sidespin serves
4. Right back-topspin serves

Step 2. Feel the motion and practice to acquire the correct form

1. Practice the same serve over and over again with multiple balls with the forehand and backhand.
2. Serve with a partner back and forth on forehand and backhand.
3. Perform the swing motion in front of mirror and compare with teacher's motion with the forehand and backhand.
4. Film the serves and get feedback from the teachers.

Step 3. Work on the consistency of forehand and backhand serves

1. Serve across the table (diagonally) with a partner or by self from the right corner of the table.
2. Serve down the table (straight) with a partner or by self from the right corner of the table.
3. Serve across the table (diagonally) with a partner or by self from the left corner of the table.
4. Serve down the table (straight) with a partner or by self from the left corner of the table.
5. Serve toward the opponent's body from left and right corners.

Step 4. Work on placements and changing lines of forehand and backhand

1. Serve from the left corner alternatively down the table, across the table, and toward the opponent's body.
2. Serve from the right corner alternatively down the table, across the table, and toward the opponent's body.

Step 5. Change speed and length of serves using above drills

1. Serve fast to make serves long.
2. Serve slowly to make serves short.
3. Serve one long and one short with identical motions.
4. Fake a long serve but make a short serve instead.
5. Fake a short serve but make a long one instead.

Step 6. Change serves using drills in above drills

1. Alternatively make flat, slice, back sidespin, and back topspin serves.
2. Serve from and toward different corners.
3. Use different speed and placement.
4. Fake a flat serve but make a spin one or reverse it.

Step 7. Serve with a partner returning using above drills

1. Serve and see how effective it is from partner's returning.
2. Serve then return partner's shot.
3. Serve to set up for attacks.

Step 8. Serve under pressure using above drills

1. Make each serve 10 times and calculate the percentage of good serves.
2. Make each serve 10 times with a partner returning and calculate the percentage of good serves.
3. Make each serve 10 times with a partner returning and calculate the percentage of good returning.
4. Use each serve in practice games and calculate the percentage of good serves.
5. Use serves alternatively in practice games and gain feedback on effectiveness.
6. Use serves in games against different players of different styles.

Practice guidelines for shots

Learning the basic shots is only the first step of learning table tennis and there is a long way between just hitting the ball and hitting effectively in games. Different opponents play different styles and they may use flat, slice, or loop shots to confuse you and it is certainly difficult to judge what kind of shots the opponent is using. Furthermore, opponents may also change speed, lines, corners, and forehand and backhand to make returns much more difficult. It is much more difficult to learn effective shots than learning serves and much more practice is certainly essential. Step-by-step practice and drills designed based on the application features in various game situation of table tennis need to be followed so that students can move from learning the basic shots into applying them in games effectively. The following guidelines provide these sequential steps and instructors and students can adopt or create drills to improve skills and their applications based on these steps. However, these steps do not make the only model for everyone. People can combine two steps together, or skip some steps, or reverse these step based on the individual needs of players. Players can and should combine the practice of shots with the practice of serving and receiving together.

Step 1. List all shots to be practiced

1. Close-table flat shots
2. Off-table flat shots
3. Snap shots
4. Lifting shots
5. Loop shots
6. Off-table backspin (slice) shots
7. Over-table backspin (chop) shots
8. Sidespin shots

Step 2. Feel the motion and practice to acquire the correct form

1. Practice the same shots over and over again on forehand and backhand fed by an instructor or a partner.
2. Rally with the instructor or a partner back and forth with forehand and backhand.
3. Perform the swing motions in front of mirror and compare with teacher's motion on forehand and backhand.
4. Film the shots and get feedback from the teachers or a partner.

Step 3. Work on the consistency of forehand and backhand shots

1. Hit forehand shots across the table (diagonally) with a partner.
2. Hit forehand shots down the table (straight) with a partner.
3. Hit backhand shots across the table (diagonally) with a partner.
4. Hit backhand shots down the table (straight) with a partner.
5. Hit toward the opponent's body.

Step 4. Work on placements and changing lines on forehand and backhand

1. Hit alternatively down the table, across the table, and toward opponent's body.
2. Hit to opponent's forehand several times and suddenly hit to the backhand.
3. Hit to opponent's backhand several times then suddenly hit to the forehand.
4. Hit with backhand several times then suddenly use backhand.

Step 5. Change speed and length of shots with a partner

    1. Hit fast to make shots long.
    2. Hit slowly to make shots short.
    3. Hit one long and one short with identical motions.
    4. Fake a long shot but make a short one instead.
    5. Fake a short shot but make a long one instead.

Step 6. Change shots using drills in above steps with a partner

    1. Alternatively make flat, slice, and topspin shots.
    2. Use different speed and placement.
    3. Slice several times then suddenly use loops.
    4. Chop continuously and suddenly use a snap shot.
    5. Backhand pushes several time then attack with a pivot shot.
    6. Partner feeds different shots then return with proper shots.

Step 7. Rally under pressure using above drills

    1. Hit each shot continuously and count how many shots were made in a rally.
    2. Play restricted games, such as flat shot and serves only (or slice only).
    3. Partner changes styles and shots in practice game and return accordingly.
    4. Change the shots and styles in the games.
    5. Use some punishment or award in the game.
    6. Play game with different players of different styles.

Practice guidelines for receiving serves

    Returning serves effectively is not easy as it looks and there is a long way between just returning the serves and returning effectively in games. The server may use flat, slice, side-backspin, or side-topspin serves to confuse you and it is certainly difficult to judge what kind of serve the opponent is using. Furthermore, the opponent may change speed, lines, corners, and forehand and backhand to make the receiving much more difficult. It is much more difficult to learn effective receiving than learning the serving and much more practice is certainly essential. Step-by-step practice and drills designed based on the application features in various game situation of table tennis need to be followed so that students can move from learning the basic receiving skills into applying them in games effectively. The following guidelines provide these sequential steps and instructors and students can adopt or create drills to improve skills and their applications based on these steps. However, these steps do not form the only model for everyone. People can combine two steps together, or skip some steps, or reverse these step based on the individual needs of players.

Step 1. List all serves to be received

    1. Flat serves
    2. Backspin (slice) serves
    3. Left back-sidespin serves
    4. Right back-topspin serves

Step 2. Learn all different shots and applications in returning serves

    1. Close-table flat shots
    2. Off-table flat shots
    3. Snap shots
    4. Lifting shots
    5. Loop shots
    6. Off-table backspin (slice) shots
    7. Over-table backspin (chop) shots
    8. Sidespin shots

Step 3. Work on judging the speed and placement of the serve and using proper movement and shots. A partner makes the same serves over and over again from and to different corners, then repeat the process with another type of serve.

    1. Move and forehand return with a proper shot across the table.
    2. Move and forehand return with a proper shot down the table.
    3. Move and backhand return with a proper shot across the table.
    4. Move and backhand return with a proper shot down the table.
    5. Return another type of serve using above drills.

Step 4. Work on the consistency of forehand and backhand returns.

    1. Continuously use forehand to return a serve across the table.
    2. Continuously use forehand to return a serve down the table.
    3. Continuously use backhand to return a serve across the table.
    4. Continuously use backhand to return a serve down the table.
    5. Return another type of serve using above drills.

Step 5. Work on placements and changing lines of forehand and backhand returns.

    1. Return with forehand alternatively down the table, across the table, and toward opponent's body.
    2. Return with backhand alternatively down the table, across the table, and toward opponent's body.
    3. The partner serves one to forehand and one to backhand. Return down the table and across the table with forehand and backhand.
    4. Return another type of serve using above drills.

Step 6. Change speed and length when returning serves

        1. Return a serve with a long shot.
        2. Return a serve with a short shot.
        3. Return across table a long shot then down the table with a short one.
        4. Return down table a short shot then across the table with a long one.
        5. Return another type of serve using above drills.

Step 7. Return serves by using different shots

        1. Return a flat serve with a flat shot, then a topspin shot.
        2. Return a slice serve with a tilt flat shot, a topspin shot, then a slice.
        3. Return a sidespin serve with a tilt flat shot, a topspin shot, then a slice.

Step 8. Return different serves when the partner alternatively changes the serves

        1. Return serves coming from different corners.
        2. Return spin and flat serves.
        3. Return left and right spin serves.
        4. Partner uses mixes up different serves and receiver tries to return accordingly.

Step 9. Return serves under pressure using above drills
        1. Calculate the percentage of good return.
        2. Use all different returns in practice games.
        3. Play game with different players of different styles.

Review questions

1. What drills should one use to improve your form in serving, receiving, and returning shots?

2. What drills should a player use to improve your consistency in serving, receiving, and returning shots?

3. What drills could one use to improve your placement in serving, receiving, and returning shots?

4. What drills should a player use to improve your ability to recognize and return different serves and shots?

5. What drills should can one use to improve your actual experience in serving, receiving, and shots?

6. What drills should may a player use to improve your ability of applying skills in serving, receiving, and shots?

7. How can a player combine serving and receiving training together?

8. Can you create new drills for your special needs?

Chapter 15

Single Game Strategies

This chapter introduces basic single game strategies. Included are general basic table tennis strategies for all players and strategies for players of different types of styles. Each style is introduced on the special features, techniques, tactics, and tips for using this style.

General basic strategies

Players of all styles use these general basic strategies. The applications of these strategies vary based on individual players. Based on these general strategies, players of different styles will further apply their specific strategies in their games.

1. Use your best serves and shots in games to ensure your best play and reduce mistakes.
2. Players can change serves and shots to keep opponent guessing what your next motion will be.
3. Change speed, power, lines and placement of the shots and serves to avoid opponent getting used to them.
4. Combine spin and flat serves to force opponent make more mistakes.
5. Attack opponent's weakness.
6. Avoid the strength of opponent. For example, hit to the backhand if the opponent is strong at forehand, or use more short chop shots if opponent is very aggressive.
7. Hit to the openings, weak side, and weak spots (such as opponent's body).

Different styles and their strategies

Players play with different styles, and each style requires specific strategies in addition to the general basic strategies. The following are basic explanations of each style.

1. Close-table fast push and attack style

Features: This style mainly uses push shots to place the ball with speed and placement and then uses forehand aggressive shots to attack. Backhand push and forehand attack players mainly use this style to deal with an aggressive opponent of the same or loop style.

Techniques: This style can use continuous backhand push and forehand attack in Photo 15.1. It can also use backhand push and pivot attack in Photo 15.2.

A. Backhand push and forehand attack (Photo 15.1)

15.1a backhand push   15.1b forehand attack

B. Backhand push and pivot attack (Photo 15.2)

15.2a push   15.2b pivot

15.2c attack

Tactics:
- Use backhand push to place the shots continuously to force mistakes
- Catch any chance to attack with strong forehand shots

Tips:
- Change lines, placements, and pace to lead the game and to create chances for smashes.
- Push opponent's backhand first then attack the forehand.
- Use power push to attack the middle to make opponent returning with weak shots then attack.

116

- Catch every chance to smash since this is the main scoring technique.
- Stay close to the table but remain flexible.
- When dealing with loop style player, stay close to the table, use quick push, powerful push and reduced-power push to control the placement. Then catch chances to smash.

2. Close-table forehand and backhand fast attacks

Features: This style uses speed and power from both forehand and backhand to attack opponent, and then create or catch chances to smash. Most time the close-table, pen-grip fast attack player like former Chinese champions use this style. Recently the tennis-grip, loop style players also use this strategy.

Techniques: Alternatively use backhand and forehand attacks continuously. When the ball is low or there is no chance to attack, use push or block shots and wait for opportunities (Photo 15.3).

15.3a forehand flat attack   15.3b backhand flat attack

Tactics:
- Attack the backhand then smash the forehand.
- Attack two corners then smash the middle.

Tips:
- Change lines and placement.
- Mainly attack opponent's backhand to create chance to smash forehand or middle.
- Catch every chance to smash.
- Stay close to the table when in offense, and stay back when in defense.
- Stay close to the table when dealing with loop style players. Use quick push to press the loop shots then use more power to smash.

3. Lift and attack

Features: This style mainly uses lifting shots to bring the ball up then attack aggressively. It is mainly used to deal with the slice, defensive type of players. This combination changes the pace of the game and force opponent to follow your playing style. Most time the close-table, pen-grip fast attack players and loop style players use this strategy against defensive players who use slices most time.

Techniques: Uses forehand or backhand high loops to lift up and use forehand or backhand smashes, flat shots, or fast loops to attack (Photo 15.4). The lifting up motion should not very powerful in case it goes too far out. On the other hand, the soft lifting shots can be smashed easily.

15.4a life a low shot   15.4b smash

Tactics:
- quick lift then smash.
- Lift to opponent's weak side.

Tips:
- Use less power for lifting shot and use more power for the smash.
- Change lines and placements to move opponent for opportunities.
- Catch every chance to smash the middle or the weak side.
- Be patient; do not smash hard if the opportunity is poor.

4. Lift, smash, and drop

Features: It combines the lifting shots and smash with drop shots. The lift, smash, and drop are usually used by the fast style players or loop style players to deal with slice type players.

Techniques: Uses forehand to lift the shots and force opponent to hit high shots. Then use forehand or backhand to smash to force opponent to stay far back, and then suddenly use a short drop when opponent is forced to stay far back away from the table (Photo 15.5).

15.5a lift the low shot   15.5b smash to force opponent back

15.5c make a drop with a chop

Tactics:

- Lift the ball carefully without much risk of being smashed.
- Catch any chances to smash.
- Make sudden drop shots after continuous smash.
- After making drop shots, be ready to catch the next opportunity.

Tips:

- Make drops when opponent is forced to stay away from the table.
- Make the drop short and low.
- Target at opponent's body when smashing if opponent is close to the table to return the drops.

5. Chop and attack

Features: This style uses short, low, quick and changing chop shots to control the game and make opponent less aggressive. Then players use quick push or snap to start the attack, and then catch every chance to smash. Players of all styles use this strategy today.

Techniques: Uses short chops shots to keep the ball low and short (over the table) and make opponent impatient and force mistakes or hit high, then use snap shots to attack any short but high shots or smash over the high but long shots (Photo 15.6).

119

15.6a chop short and low   15.6b snap at high shots

Tactics:
- Use short chops continuously.
- Catch chances to use snap or smash.
- Change lines and speed of the chops.

Tips:
- Be patient and wait for the good opportunities.
- Start attacks as early as possible.
- Catch every good chance to smash.
- Make chops short and low so that opponent cannot attack first.

6. Slice and attack

Features: It combines slice and attacking shots together. It usually uses long slice shots to corners to make opponent stay away from the table and less aggressive, and then catch or create chances for attacks. It can also use consistent, low, and changing slice shots to force opponent to lift while in move then attack back. Most defensive players use this strategy.

Techniques: Use long slice shots to keep the ball low but long or short and make opponent impatient and make mistakes or hit high, then use smash of loop shots to attack any high shots (Photo 15.7).

15.7a slice long and low   15.7b attach with forehand shots

Tactics:

- Use long slice to the backhand corner, then use forehand to attack.
- Use long slices to hit two corners to make opponent move then attack.
- Use long slices and short chops to confuse the opponent.

Tips:

- Combine spin and flat shots to make the opponent hit high.
- Keep the slice low to avoid smashes.
- Make opponent move side to side, or back and forth, and then catch chances to attack.

7. Serve and attack

Features: It mainly changes the patterns (spin or flat), lines, placements, and speed of serves to force the opponent to hit back with weak returns or make mistakes. Then the serve can take advantage of the weak returns or mistakes. The strategy focuses on the first three shots to control the game and to score. This strategy was used by fast style players but nowadays is used by most players.

Techniques: Uses various serves of flat and spins at different speed, spin, power, and placement from different corners to force opponent make mistakes, and then catch any opportunities to attack when the opponent's return is not good. Whenever finding which serve(s) opponent does not return well, you should keep using it until the opponent adapts to it (Photo 15.8).

15.8a use a side-top spin serves   15.8b backhand fast loop attack

Tactics:

- Combine spin and flat serve together.
- Use fast serves to attack both corners.
- Use short serves to make opponent to lift up then attack.
- Keep identical motions when using different serves.
- Use different serves to keep opponent guessing and under pressure.

Tips:

- Move opponent with different serves to different corners.

- Be ready to attack after the serve.
- Know how opponent will return each serve for better preparation.

8. Loop with forehand and backhand

Features: It mainly use loop shots to force opponent to back up away from the table and return high or fast loops. This style forces opponent to change their original patterns and rhythms and to follow the loop player on long and high shots which they do not like. Then the serve can take advantage of the weak returns or mistakes. This is an effective style to deal with slice type of players. This style is also often combined with the close table fast-attack style to control both the close-table and off-table plays.

Techniques: Use both fast and high loops with forehand and backhand on serves and shots. If combined with the fast-attack style, also use close table pushes, flat shots, and other skills (Photo 15.9).

15.9a forehand loop   15.9b backhand loop

Tactics:
- Use loops whenever there is a chance
- Change high and fast loops to confuse opponent
- Force opponent to follow your rhythm and pace
- Keep identical motions when using different loops
- Use different loops and other shots to keep opponent guessing and under pressure.

Tips:
- Change lines and paces
- Attack opponent's body and away from opponent
- Catch every chance to smash.

Review questions

1. What are the basic single game strategies?
2. How does a close-table push and attack style player play?

3. What skills should a player perform well if he/she wants to be a forehand and backhand attack style player?
4. How does one apply the lift and attack strategies in single games?
5. How does the lift, smash, and drop style strategy work?
6. What are the tactics to play the chop and attack strategy effectively?
7. What is the common way to play the slice and attack style?
8. How should a player apply the serve and attack style in single games?
9. Why should the loop style combine with close-table fast style?

Chapter 16

Double game strategies

This chapter introduces basic table tennis double game strategies. Included are pairing patterns, rotation patterns of the two players, and tips for teamwork and strategies.

Pairing

There are different pairing patterns for table tennis. Each pairing pattern has unique characteristics and players should try and find their best partner.

1. Both players of the same styles. This pairing can make both players work together very well. Examples include two fast style players, two slice style players, or two loop players.
2. Two players of different styles. This pairing can confuse opponents and make it difficult for opponents to get used to the changes. Examples include one fast style player and one loop player, or a loop player and a slice player.
3. One right-handed and one left-handed style. This pairing can reduce the movement and avoid bumping into each other.
4. One close table player and one off-table player. This pairing can reduce the chances of bumping, and make up each other's weakness. Examples include one close-table fast style player and a middle range loop player, or a fast style player and an off-table slice player.

Rotations

In a doubles game, the players have to take turns hitting the ball with their partner. After each shot, a player has to move out so that the partner can get into the best position for the next shot. It is very important that both players establish an effective rotation pattern and alternative rotation patterns.

1. Circular Rotations (Figure 16.1)

Each player moves in a circular way behind the partner after each shot and should be ready to move up and hit. Both players move the same way and two left-handed or right-handed aggressive players can use this movement.

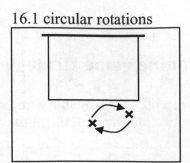

16.1 circular rotations

2. Up and Down Rotations (Figure 16.2)

Each player moves toward table in a diagonal way to return a shot then back up the same way. One left-handed and one right-handed pair use this rotation.

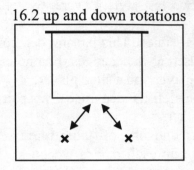

16.2 up and down rotations

3. T-Rotations (Figure 16.3)

The front person moves sideways and the back person moves back and forth. Mostly pairs of one fast style player (front) and one loop style player (back), or one close-table offensive player (front) and one slice style player (back) use this rotation.

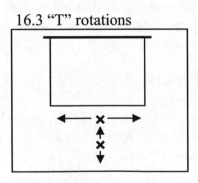

16.3 "T" rotations

4. Triangle Rotations (Figure 16.4)

Each player using this rotation pattern moves to sides to return shot, then step back to the middle for the next shot in a triangle way. It is used often to return angles shots to sides and it is similar to the circular rotation.

16.4 triangle rotations

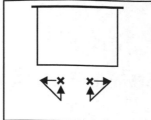

Teamwork and Strategies

1. Establish a good rotation and movement patterns.
2. Create chances for your partner when returning a shot or serve.
3. Cover your partner's weaknesses.
4. Attack the weaker opponent.
5. Hit to the opponent who just finished the shot and is moving away.
6. Use your best serves and shots in games to ensure your best play and reduce mistakes.
7. Change serves and shots to keep opponents guessing what the next motion will be.
8. Change speed, power, lines and placement of the shots and serves to avoid opponents adapting to them.
9. Combine spin and flat serves to force opponent make more mistakes.
10. Attack opponents' weaknesses.
11. Avoid the strength of opponent. For example, hit to the backhand if opponent is strong at forehand, or use more short chop shots if opponent is very aggressive.
12. Hit to the openings, weak side, and an opponent's body.

Review Questions

1. What are the basic paring patterns in doubles games?
2. What kinds of couples tend to use the circular rotation?
3. What kinds of couples tend to use the up and down rotation?
4. What kinds of couples tend to use T-rotation?
5. What kinds of couples tend to use triangle rotation?
6. What are the common kinds of teamwork and strategies in double games?

Appendix

Available websites of worldwide table tennis associations

USATT http://www.usatt.org
International Table Tennis Federation http://www.ittf.com

Australia   tta@nswscd.com.au
Austria http://www.oettv.org
Belarus http://bttf.bsu.by
Brazil http://www.cbtm.org.br
Bulgaria bttf@abv.bg
Canada http://www.ctta.ca
Chile http://www.fechiteme.cl
China http://www.ctta.com.cn
Chinese Tai Pei cttta@libra.seed.net.tw
Costa Rica faguilar@cita.ucr.ac.cr
Croatia hsts@zg.hinet.hr
Czech ctta@fws.cstv.cz
Denmark http://www.dbtu.dk
Egypt http://www.egypttta.com
England http://www.etta.co.uk
Finland office@sptl.slu.fi
France http://www.fftt.com
Germany http://www.tischtennis.de
Greece http://www.httf.gr
Hong Kong http://www.hktta.org.hk
Hungary http://www.moatsz.hu
Iceland http://www.toto.is.sersamb/bti
India ttfi@vsnl.com
Indonesia farid-r@centrin.net.id
Iran info@iranttf.com
Iraq inoc@nisciraq.net
Ireland http://www.ttireland.com

Israel http://www.tabletennis.co.il
Italy http://www.fitet.org
Japan http://www.jtta.or.jp
Kenya mediaplus@net2000ke.com
Khosovo http://www.fppk.com
Korea gfasa@silibank.com
Korea tabletennis@sports.or.kr
Malaysia ttam@tm.net.my
Malta http://www.mtta.net
Mexico femeteme@netservice.com.mx
Netherlands bondsbureau@nttb.nl
New Zealand http://www.tabletennis.org.nz
Pakistan gymkhana@wol.net.pk
Peru mmack@terra.com.pe
Philippines president@tatap.com
Poland http://www.pzts.pl
Romania frtenismasa@mcit.ro
Russia fntr@roc.ru
Singapore http://sgtta.org
Slovenia http://www.nt-zveza.si
South Africa http://www.tabletennis.co.za
Spain http://www.rfetm.com
Sweden http://www.svenskbordtennis.com
Switzerland http://www.sttv.ch
Thailand http://www.ttat.org
Wales http://www.btinternet.com/~ttaw